The Declaration of America

Other Books of Interest from St. Augustine's Press

Will Morrisey, *Herman Melville's Ship of State*

Ellis Sandoz, *Give Me Liberty: Studies in Constitutionalism and Philosophy*

Ellis Sandoz, *The Politics of Truth and Other Untimely Essays: The Crisis of Civic Consciousness*

Pierre Manent, *Seeing Things Politically: Interviews with Benedicte Delorme-Montini*

David Lowenthal, *Slave State: Rereading Orwell's 1984*

Marvin R. O'Connell, *Telling Stories that Matter: Memoirs and Essays*

Josef Pieper, *Exercises in the Elements: Essays–Speeches–Notes*

Josef Pieper, *A Journey to Point Omega: Autobiography from 1964*

Joseph Bottum, *The Decline of the Novel*

Jeremy Black, *The Importance of Being Poirot*

Jeremy Black, *In Fielding's Wake*

Jeremy Black, *Smollett's Britain*

D. Q. McInerny, *Being Ethical*

Roger Scruton, *An Intelligent Person's Guide to Modern Culture*

Roger Scruton, *The Meaning of Conservatism: Revised 3rd Edition*

Roger Scruton, *The Politics of Culture and Other Essays*

Roger Scruton, *On Hunting*

Anne Drury Hall, *Where the Muses Still Haunt*

John Poch, *God's Poems: The Beauty of Poetry and the Christian Imagination*

René Girard, *A Theater of Envy: William Shakespeare*

Marion Montgomery, *With Walker Percy at the Tupperware Party*

Gene Fendt, *Camus' Plague: Myth for Our World*

Frederic Raphael and Joseph Epstein, *Where Were We?: The Conversation Continues*

Winston S. Churchill, *The River War*

The Declaration of America
Our Principles in Thought and Action

RICHARD FERRIER

ST. AUGUSTINE'S PRESS
South Bend, Indiana

Manufactured in the United States of America.

1 2 3 4 5 6 28 27 26 25 24 23

Library of Congress Control Number: 2022939151

Paperback ISBN: 978-1-58731-203-8
Ebook ISBN: 978-1-58731-204-5

∞ The paper used in this publication meets the minimum requirements of the American National Standard for Information Sciences – Permanence of Paper for Printed Materials, ANSI Z39.48-1984.

St. Augustine's Press
www.staugustine.net

TABLE OF CONTENTS

AUTHOR'S INTRODUCTION

The seed for this book was sown in 1996, when my colleague David Quackenbush and I became ardent volunteers in Alan Keyes' campaign for the Republican nomination for President. He taught us to see what President Lincoln saw 160 years ago: An American should always take his principles and form his sentiments from those expressed in the Declaration of Independence.

Another colleague and I developed a curriculum and textbook which we called, "Declaration Statesmanship." A few schools and many homeschooling families used that book over the 20 years since then.

The present book uses much of the content of that textbook, revised for a general audience. A number of passages were rewritten or omitted, and errors of fact were corrected. Some new developments from the past two decades were acknowledged.

Besides the debt of gratitude I owe to Dr. Seeley for his collaboration on the textbook, I'd like to thank my friend Dr. Michael Platt, whose advice on style and whose analysis of the structure of the Declaration were of great help to me.

There would not be such a book at all without innumerable gifts of editing, clerical matters of all kinds, and patient and loving support from my wife, Kathy.

CHAPTER 1
THE DECLARATION OF AMERICA

Let us compare the Declaration of Independence to a marriage.

A marriage is a covenant, or as the law has it, a contract, and that contract is made when the couple DECLARES that it is one. It is this day that they celebrate as their anniversary. They date the years of their marriage from this day. And their obligations are most especially the ones they make on this day. "Forsaking all others ... in sickness and in health ... till death do us part. So help us God."

How old is our Republic? What day do we celebrate as its anniversary? Abraham Lincoln pointed to the answers in the Gettysburg Address, given in 1863. "Fourscore and seven years ago our fathers brought forth on this continent a new nation...." *Fourscore and seven*, that is, eighty-seven. 1863 minus 87 equals 1776. Not the day when George Washington submitted the text of the Constitution to Congress, September 17th, 1787, nor the date New Hampshire's ratification made it come into force, nor when reluctant Rhode Island made it unanimous. Not Paul Revere's ride or the battle of Bunker Hill, both in 1775. No, none of these, but the "Glorious Fourth," as Lincoln and many others have called it. July 4th, 1776. The date of the Declaration.

We even made a "family emblem" for ourselves, or rather, started to design one, on the same Fourth of July. You can see it on our dollar bill. It is called, "The Great Seal of the United States."[1] Here is what the U.S. Department of State says about it:

> Before it adjourned on July 4, 1776, the Continental Congress of the newly independent United States passed a resolution:

1 http://www.state.gov/documents/organization/27807.pdf.

> *Resolved, that Dr. Franklin, Mr. J. Adams and Mr. Jefferson, be a committee, to bring in a device for a seal for the United States of America.*
>
> Thus, three of the five men who had drafted the Declaration of Independence were brought together in further service to their country. The revolutionaries needed an emblem and national coat of arms to give visible evidence of a sovereign nation...."
>
> When the final design was adopted by Congress in 1782, Charles Thomson, Secretary to Congress wrote that the shield signified, "... the several states all joined in one solid compact entire," and that "The motto alludes to this union." He added that "The constellation denotes a new state taking its place and rank among other sovereign powers." And he concluded that, "The date underneath is that of the Declaration of Independence and the words under it (*novus ordo seclorum*) signify the beginning of the New American Era, which commences from that date."
>
> The national motto, found on the Seal, "E Pluribus Unum," further manifests that the American Union springs from the Declaration, as does Jefferson's resolution as a board member of the University of Virginia in 1825: "[the best guides to the principles of the United States are] The Declaration of Independence, as the fundamental act of union of these States...."

The comparison of a nation to a marriage is especially strong in the case of the United States. Unlike most other nations, such as France or England, and like all marriages, our nation came into being as a deliberate act. Before the Declaration, there were thirteen colonies. Afterwards, we were one People. We made war as one, entered into treaties as one, and made our principles known to a watching world. The Declaration states that we are "one people" who "assume ... the separate and equal station to which the laws of nature and of nature's God entitle them."

Our union begun by the Declaration has been a great blessing. Some marriages are so successful that they become an example to other couples. We live in a nation that has been an example to other nations. As ancient

Rome was widely admired for its peace and stability, the United States has become a symbol of liberty and justice to oppressed peoples. When Chinese demonstrators for freedom faced the tanks in Tiananmen Square, they erected a model of the Statue of Liberty to inspire them. As we write these words in 2020, great crowds in Hong Kong wave our flag in defiance of the despots who rule China.

Marriages have their ups and downs. When times are tough, good friends or counselors might remind couples of their solemn vows, of what they pledged to each other and before their friends and their God. You could say that the founding principle of the marriage, the spirit that they try to live out day by day, is contained in those vows and the ceremony surrounding them on that special day in which the marriage was made. The same has been true in our political union.

Lincoln said, in Independence Hall, on his way to Washington D.C. to be inaugurated as President of the United States, that he "never had a feeling politically that did not spring from the sentiments embodied in the Declaration of Independence." Sixty-five years later, in that same Hall, another American president, Calvin Coolidge, said:

> It was not because it was proposed to establish a new nation, but because it was proposed to establish a new nation *on new principles*, that July 4, 1776 has come to be regarded as one of the greatest days in history.
> – Speech on the occasion of the 150th anniversary of the Declaration

What were these new principles? A brief answer may be found in the first of the *Federalist Papers*, a series of essays published in the newspapers of New York from 1787–88. John Jay, Alexander Hamilton, and James Madison, using the pseudonym "Publius," argued in these essays for the adoption of the Constitution. In the first Federalist paper, Publius wrote,

> ... it seems to have been reserved to the people of this country, by their conduct and example, to decide whether societies of men are really capable or not of establishing good government from reflection and choice, or whether they are forever destined

> to depend for their political constitutions on accident and force.
> – *Federalist 1*

Publius meant that America would enshrine Liberty. The people would rule by their own choice. But he also meant that that choice would be reasonable. It would come from "reflection." On what would the people reflect? The answer is given early in the Declaration itself. "The Laws of Nature and of Nature's God," and the "inalienable rights" to "life, liberty, and the pursuit of happiness."

In summary, the Declaration founded America and gave it its fundamental principles. The nation so founded was seen by its founders and the whole world as a trial of the ability of a free people to establish a deliberately chosen form of government in accordance with the laws of nature and of nature's God. The basis of that government would be the authority of the people, coming from their endowment, by their Creator, with inalienable rights.

CHAPTER 2
A LOOK BACKWARDS

You are not reading a history book, but a study of the meaning, truth, and power of the principles of the American Republic. Still, a bit of history will be in order here. It will help us read the Declaration in the next three chapters, and it will shed a bit of light on why the first modern republican nation was brought forth here, in America, in 1776.

On June 10, 1776, the Second Continental Congress charged Thomas Jefferson, John Adams, Benjamin Franklin, Roger Sherman and Robert Livingston with the task of drafting a Declaration of Independence. Congress officially declared independence on July 2, and accepted the committee's Declaration, with some significant alterations, on July 4.[2]

By this time, the colonies had been engaged in armed conflict with British troops for over a year, since the famous April, 1775, engagements at Lexington and Concord in Massachusetts. A Continental Army of 18,000 men, with George Washington as Commander-in-Chief, had driven the British out of Boston, and was then facing a new Royal force in and around New York City; colonial troops had captured British forts in upper New York; Americans had even attempted to seize Quebec and Montreal in Canada. All this before the actual Declaration of Independence.

Why did Congress take so long to declare independence? And what had brought about the fighting in the first place?

WHO MAKES THE LAWS? The Colonies vs. Parliament

The short answer to the second question is this: Britain would not relinquish its claim to make laws for America, and the Americans would not acknowledge such a claim as right.

Beginning in 1764, the British government, burdened with debts, including costs from the recent French and Indian War in America, had

2 https://www.archives.gov/founding-docs/declaration/how-did-it-happen.

decided to raise money by placing taxes on the colonies. While the two peoples had benefited financially from their relationship for over a century, Parliament had never tried to tax the colonies directly. In 1765, they broke with this precedent of restraint, and passed the Stamp Act, a direct tax.

Four years earlier, the government across the Atlantic had extended the powers of the Royal army and navy to search and seize colonial properties in an effort to repress smugglers. As a further measure of enforcement, it had provided for a permanent British military presence in the colonies, and insisted that the colonial legislatures pay for the troops.

When the colonies offered resolute, united, and mostly peaceful opposition, including a boycott of British goods, Parliament, urged to conciliate by King George III, backed down, repealing the Stamp Act in March of 1766. But it remained adamant that it had the right to tax, and, indeed, to make any laws for the colonies it wished. As it repealed the Stamp Act, Parliament declared:

> ... the King's majesty by and with the advice and consent of the lords spiritual and temporal, and commons of Great Britain, in parliament assembled, had, hath, and of right ought to have, full power and authority to make laws and statutes of sufficient force and validity to bind the colonies in all cases whatsoever....
> – Quoted from *The Rebirth of Liberty*, Clarence B. Carson

The Americans were pleased to be relieved of the burden of the taxes and other measures; the right to impose them they never granted. Ten years later, they were to shed their blood to vindicate their view.

Tension was renewed when Parliament insisted that the colonists buy taxed tea from the British East India Company. The colonists not only refused to pay the tax; they refused to let the ships land the tea. In Boston, colonists went so far as to board the ships and throw the tea overboard. Parliament decided it was time to teach the Americans a lesson. In 1774, revealing their intention, they passed what they called the Coercive Acts. The colonists called them the Intolerable Acts. The port of Boston was to be closed until the tea was paid for, effectively shutting down Boston's economy; Massachusetts' legislature was suspended, and local council meetings were limited; American officials who didn't comply were to be tried only in England; and colonists were ordered to receive British troops into their homes.

While Massachusetts was the most directly affected by these measures, the other colonies realized that the same could easily happen to them. (New York also had had its legislature suspended for resisting the Quartering Act.) So twelve colonies sent representatives to what became known as the First Continental Congress. While petitioning the British government to repeal the Coercive Acts, the Congress encouraged the people of Massachusetts to form their own government and to organize a militia in order to resist the measures with force, if necessary. They laid the foundations for a united colonial government to resist the measures. They also published a declaration of their own:

> That the inhabitants of the English colonies in North America, by the immutable laws of nature, the principles of the English Constitution,[3] and the several charters or compacts ... are entitled to life, liberty, and property, and they have never ceded to any sovereign power whatever, a right to dispose either without their consent.
> – Declaration of the First Continental Congress, from *The Rebirth of Liberty*, Carson

Parliament soon declared some of the colonies to be in a state of rebellion, and ordered the army to seize military supplies. This led to the fighting at Lexington and Concord. The Second Continental Congress met the next month, in May 1775. Besides taking charge of a coordinated continental military resistance, Congress also sent one more petition to the King. This appeal was known as the *Olive Branch Petition*, so-called because of its peaceful and moderate tone, and its expressions of respect for the King and the ties that bound the Americans and their British kin.

3 When the colonists referred to the English "Constitution," they were not thinking of a written document like ours. The English never had, and still do not have, a written constitution. The English "constitution" is the body of English common law and mostly unwritten customs according to which they govern themselves, along with a few important, traditional documents like the Magna Carta and the Bill of Rights of 1688.

The King refused even to receive the petition. His answer was in deeds; he declared the colonies out of his protection, his Parliament prohibited trade with them and declared their vessels lawful prize and their seamen liable to impressment into the Royal Navy. In January 1776, after a group of patriots had driven the Royal governor, Lord Dunsmore, out of town, the British bombarded and burned Norfolk, Virginia. Or so went the American side of the story. The British claimed that the Americans burned the town themselves, to prevent the British from obtaining supplies for use against the colonies. Dunsmore, it ought to be noted, had angered and terrified the Virginians by trying to induce their slaves and indentured servants to desert them in exchange for freedom and protection by the British forces. The offer was taken by few, but the memory of it, and the threat it posed, lived long in Southern minds, and was to show up among the charges against the King in the Declaration of Independence.

There was no dispute about a similar incident, which took place in October of 1775, at Falmouth (now Portland), Maine. Provoked by rowdy patriots, the captain of the 16-gun vessel, *Canceaux*, bombarded the town with heated shot, destroying it in the ensuing fire.

HESITATIONS

Even so, with lines drawn firmly and military action escalating, with colonies setting up their own governments, and Congress acting as a government of the United Colonies, formal declaration of independence had to wait for over six months after the burning of Norfolk. This is an indication of how loath the colonists were to break with England and King George. The colonists had many ties to England. Most had family still in Britain. They were proud to be subjects of the British king. The colonists were generally happy with their lives, and with the peace and prosperity they enjoyed in their new land. If they separated from England and King George, then who would be their new head of state? Would they make someone King? They had no one with a plausible claim to be King. The colonies never even had a nobility from whom they might choose a king. Though they foresaw it only partially, a republic or democracy, some form of popular government, was the most likely outcome of separation. And they had little desire at first to cast themselves upon the unknown waters of democracy, which they associated with instability and turmoil.

A look back on the history of unlimited democracy, with which educated colonists were very familiar, would give them reason to doubt that it offered any hope of a better situation.

LIBERTY AND REPUBLICAN GOVERNMENTS IN THE ANCIENT AND MEDIEVAL WORLD

The city-state of Athens was preeminent among a number of democracies that flourished in the ancient world. At the height of its glory it was home to the great tragedians, Aeschylus, Sophocles and Euripides. Socrates, the father of Western philosophy, was an Athenian. The city was rich in arts and commerce and, for a time, deployed the greatest military and naval power in the Mediterranean.

Pericles was the principal political leader of Athens in its glory days, and its chief strategist during the first years of the Peloponnesian War. This is what he said in his famous *Funeral Oration*:

> Our constitution does not copy the laws of neighboring states; we are rather a pattern to others than imitators ourselves. Its administration favors the many instead of the few; this is why it is called a democracy. If we look to the laws, they afford equal justice to all in their private differences; if to social standing, advancement in public life falls to reputation for capacity, class considerations not being allowed to interfere with merit; nor again does poverty bar the way, if a man is able to serve the state, he is not hindered by the obscurity of his condition.
> – Thucydides, *The Peloponnesian War*, Book II

These are sweet words. But they are made less savory by sour facts. Consider:

1. The same Athenian democracy that reared Socrates put him to death for calling into question its polytheistic state religion.
2. The wealth and culture of the city was based on extensive use of slavery. Slaves outnumbered free citizens.
3. Athens acquired an empire which it ruled more and more by force. Pericles, speaking to the Assembly less than a year after his Funeral Oration,

said of that empire, "... to recede is no longer possible, if indeed any of you has become enamored of the honesty of such an unambitious part. For what you hold is, to speak somewhat plainly, a tyranny; to take it was perhaps wrong, but to let it go is unsafe." Fourteen years after this speech, the Athenians attacked the little island of Melos, a neutral city in the great war that had engulfed all Greece. When they took the city, they captured and put to death all the male citizens, and enslaved the women and children. As evidenced by their treatment of the Melians and other subjects in their empire, not to mention their use of slaves, the Athenians also did not think that freedom was the proper or natural condition of all men. That it was the proper condition of Athenian citizens, they had no doubt. But it was not right for other men, if their subjection could be beneficial for Athens.

4. Pericles himself admits that democracy favors "the many," that is, a part, a faction of the free men. Though he speaks of equal justice, in fact the city was riven by factional politics, the wealthy faced off with the democrats and there were two coups of the wealthy and two democratic restorations in less than thirty years after his death. The City's general popular sovereignty was not moderated by a written constitution setting up checks and balances to ensure the rights of holders of large properties and other minorities. This meant not only that Athenian democracy was prone to acts of tyranny over innocent foreigners like the Melians, but that it was prone to what James Madison, among others, was to call "the tyranny of the majority."
5. The power and glory of the Athenians lasted only briefly, and was marred by the factions, rash and unjust military aggression, and civil wars that we touch on above; and in the end, the city was conquered by its enemies and faded from prominence. In its most ambitious aggression, the expedition against Syracuse in Sicily, the populist faction, "the many," then in charge, showed enormous energy, but a near complete lack of good judgment. In short, Athens fell from greatness by gross defects in prudence and justice.
6. What was true of Athens was true of the ancient democracies generally. All had a state religion. None had adequate checks against the tyranny of the majority. All were scarred by civil conflicts and disorders. All were based on slavery and prone to injure the rights of the wealthy.

> Plato, who grew up in Imperial Athens, places Democracy near the bottom of his list ranking regimes, just above Tyranny, and his student, Aristotle, the other great political philosopher of antiquity, listed Democracy, along with Oligarchy and Tyranny, among the three forms of unjust or corrupt government in his *Politics*.

A similar tale could be told of the petty republics of medieval Italy. Florence is perhaps the most glorious, and at the same time, disheartening instance. The city was rich and cultured. Like Athens, it gave great names to the story of civilization, most notably the author of the *Divine Comedy*, Dante. But, as readers of that work will recall, Dante's city was torn apart by civil strife; some of the worst actors in that tragedy dot the lower circles of his *Inferno*. Dante himself spent the end of his life in bitter exile, and his experience of mismanaged civic liberty led him to write a treatise in favor of large imperial political rule, the *De Monarchia*.

We do not mean to say that the actual monarchies, aristocracies, or oligarchies of medieval or ancient times were models of justice and peace, only that the record of the democratic or republican government, which was also called "popular government," was sufficiently bad to lead Publius to write,

> The instability, injustice, and confusion introduced into the public councils have, in truth, been the mortal diseases under which popular governments have everywhere perished; as they continue to be the favorite and fruitful topics from which the adversaries to liberty derive their most specious declamations.
> – *Federalist 10*

Thus the facts and the judgment of such astute observers as James Madison, who was probably the real author of *Federalist 10*, led sensible men to doubt the capacity of free men to govern themselves, at least as the old city states like Florence and Athens did. Something new was needed to remove these doubts: "*novus ordo seclorum.*"

REASONS FOR INDEPENDENCE

"Did you take up arms against intolerable oppressions?
"Oppressions? I didn't feel them."

> *"What, were you not oppressed by the Stamp Act?"*
> *"I never saw one of those stamps. I certainly never paid a penny for one of them."*
> *"Well, what then about the tea tax?"*
> *"I never drank a drop of the stuff; the boys threw it all overboard."*
> *"Then I suppose you had been reading Harrington or Sidney or Locke about the eternal principles of liberty?"*
> *"Never heard of 'em. We read only the Bible, the Catechism, Watts' Psalms and Hymns, and the Almanac."*
> *"Well, then, what was the matter? And what did you mean in going to the fight?"*
> *"Young man, what we meant in going for those redcoats was this:* ***We always had governed ourselves, and we always meant to. They didn't mean we should."***
> – From a conversation between Judge Mellen Chamberlain and the then 91 year old Captain Preston, a veteran of Concord, reported in Morrison's *Oxford History of the American People*, pp. 212–3

Why did the colonists finally decide to break with motherland and monarch? A thorough attempt at an explanation would be very long. We only examine two of the causes here. First, the Americans lost faith in King George; they came to believe that he was a tyrant trying to rob them of their freedom. And second, they became convinced that they could do without a king. Or, to put this second cause positively, they came to have hope in the possibility of just and stable popular government. We will look briefly at each of these factors.

THE BRITISH HISTORY OF RESISTING TYRANTS

Let's look first at the reasons the Americans came to mistrust the king. Before Henry VIII, English kings had always been limited in what they could do by their dependence on the landed aristocracy and the leaders of important towns, as well as by the independence of the Catholic Church, which could criticize their actions and impose certain penalties on them.

One important way in which the king was dependent on his subjects was taxation. For centuries it had been the case that, if the king wanted to institute new taxes in order to raise more money, he had to get the authorization of Parliament. Parliament was a body consisting of nobles, clergy and representatives of important towns. If the king wanted to wage war, increase the number of his personal troops or institute new offices, he could, as long as he could fund these ventures from his personal properties or through taxes already in existence. But if he needed more money, he had to get the Parliament to agree. In time Parliament came to have a more active role in government, giving counsel to the king, proposing and discussing the merits of new laws. Even if the king didn't need to raise more money, the nobles and bishops were sufficiently independent and powerful to check royal ventures that might endanger the commonwealth over which he ruled.

The monarchs in the sixteenth century, especially Henry VIII, broke through many of these barriers. Henry intimidated the nobles and commons in Parliament through extensive prosecutions for treason and other crimes. Those who got in his way faced loss of titles and property, imprisonment, and, in many cases, death. He also subjected the bishops by having himself proclaimed head of the English Church. When English subjects went to America in the early seventeenth century, they were removed from much direct interference by the king. He remained the head of government, an office which he exercised, not very forcefully, through appointed governors in many colonies. But the role of Parliament, which included a share in making laws and approving taxation, was taken over by local townships and colonial assemblies. Over the century and a half before the Declaration of Independence, the colonial assemblies acquired an ever-greater role in American legislation. Moreover, a much larger percentage of the free adult males had voting rights in America than in Britain. Accordingly, during this time, the colonists were more self-governing than their brethren who remained in England.

In the mother country, the seventeenth century witnessed two major struggles for power between the king and Parliament. Parliament won both battles, forcibly removing two kings from office. The second of these, known [by the winners!] as the Glorious Revolution, ended with the removal of King James II. The Glorious Revolution was received with joy in America, in part because James II, breaking with the tolerant policy of previous monarchs, had begun to usurp local self-government in New England

and New York. These usurpations were cut short by his overthrow in 1688–89. Parliament replaced him with William and Mary, and at the same time passed the English Bill of Rights. It was quite clear that under this new regime Parliament had the greater authority.

The new balance of power between the king and Parliament caused a difficulty with the colonies, one that did not become evident until the middle of the eighteenth century. At that time, Parliament began to claim an authority over the colonies even greater than the king, acting through his governors, had exercised. As we have seen, they tried to tax the colonies directly. After all, they had the power to tax in Britain; should they not have the power to tax in the colonies as well?

The colonists resisted this notion with all their might. Their experience, the experience of Britain over centuries, had taught them that they must have a role in deciding what taxes would be laid on them. Under the king's governors, they had this authority, as well as a major influence on all other legislation that affected them. If Parliament in Britain could make laws and impose taxes without their counsel or consent, they would have no lawful means to prevent themselves from being used for the advantage of those across the Atlantic in Britain. King or Parliament, it made no difference. If those directly affected by laws had no role in making them, then they would be little better than servants of distant masters.

Although the initial conflict was directly with Parliament, the actions of the king towards the end of 1775 had led some of the colonists to believe that he was encouraging, even directing Parliament, in its actions. King George III had refused to hear the *Olive Branch Petition*, his governors and captains had engaged in military and naval action, and concurrently, Parliament had begun to treat the Americans as open rebels. Before this time, Americans had placed their trust in, and given expressions of their loyalty to their monarch, and complained of a corrupt and overreaching Parliament. Now, as they hesitated at the brink of independence, they were faced with the humiliating prospect of admitting, and professing, that they had been in error. Perhaps the king was not their friend and prop, their remaining hope for continued union with the mother country. Perhaps he was a tyrant.

In the beginning of the year 1776, an unknown young writer, brought to America by Ben Franklin, published a pamphlet called *Common Sense.*

His name was Tom Paine. *Common Sense* circulated very rapidly throughout America. In it Paine argued that not only was King George the cause of the troubles with Britain, but also that having a king at all was ungrounded in revelation and reason, and inimical to liberty. And he argued, in the most forceful and persuasive terms, that the time for independence, for separation, was now.

A few brief citations will give the taste, and the fire, of Paine's pamphlet:

> – Government by Kings was first introduced into the world by the heathens, from whom the children of Israel copied the custom. It was the most preposterous invention the Devil ever set on foot for the promotion of idolatry. The heathens paid divine honors to their deceased Kings, and the Christian world hath improved on the plan by doing the same to their living ones. How impious is the title of sacred Majesty applied to a worm, who in the midst of his splendor is crumbling into the dust!
> – A thirst for Absolute power is the natural disease of monarchy.
> – We have it in our power to begin the world over again. A situation, similar to the present, has not happened since the days of Noah until now. The birthday of a new world is at hand, and a race of men, perhaps as numerous as all Europe contains, are to receive their portion of freedom from the event of a few months.
> – Thomas Paine, *Common Sense*, 1776

Within months of the publication of this pamphlet, numerous local initiatives were passed calling for independence. George Washington, commanding the Colonial forces at Boston, ceased thinking of the hostile army before him as the "Ministerial Army," meaning by that phrase, "the army of The Prime Minister of Parliament," and began to see it as the Royal Army, or the British Army. He wrote a friend: "A few more of such flaming arguments, as were exhibited at Falmouth and Norfolk, added to the sound doctrine and unanswerable reasoning contained in the pamphlet *Common Sense*, will not leave numbers at a loss to decide on the propriety of a separation." The pamphlet's sales were estimated as high as 100,000 copies, in a nation of perhaps two million readers. Rarely has a political book so met the needs of the time—a time calling for humanity, in the American People, to make the trial of an independent, popular government.

DARING THE RISK OF DEMOCRACY

So, Americans had come to think of King George III as a tyrant. What made them have confidence in popular government as the alternative? We would suggest three answers: experience, reason, and religion. And the three are related.

Let's start with experience. Although the Americans had no experience of exercising the full range of sovereign power—they had not made treaties with the European states, or regulated their foreign commerce, or gone to war independently of the mother country—most colonies had experienced more than a century of local self-government. They had learned the craft of legislation and the art of compromise in the school of political practice here in the New World. And, on the whole, they had governed themselves prudently. This experience was not limited to the township and the colonial assemblies. The forms of Protestant religion they held to also gave them experience in self-government, of the congregation or other units of the body of believers. This was most especially true in New England. Alexis de Tocqueville puts it this way:

> The greatest part of English America has been peopled by men who, after having escaped the authority of the pope, did not submit to any religious supremacy; they therefore brought to the New World a Christianity that I cannot depict better than to call it democratic and republican: this singularly favors the establishment of a republic and of democracy in affairs. From the beginning, politics and religion were in accord, and they have not ceased to be so since.
> – *Democracy in America, Vol. I, Part 2, Ch. 9*

Religious and political experience, and the lessons gained from them, were supplemented by two other causes. One was human reason, in particular, the political works of a number of English and French writers of the seventeenth and eighteenth centuries, the most prominent of whom was John Locke. These authors taught that all men are naturally equal, and they had theorized about political regimes, including democracies, founded on consent, or contract, between those who would live under the laws of the state.

The age in which Locke and others wrote was a time of great confidence in human reason. Isaac Newton and others had made astonishing advances in mathematics and natural science. The seminal technology for the Industrial Age was appearing, navigation improved, the whole Western World was confident in the new powers that the new science, "the Scientific Revolution" had given mankind. So, the Americans, for their part, dared to hope in a new political science that would overcome the flaws of the popular governments of the past.

The other, undoubtedly more important, influence was the Bible. In I Samuel 7, when the elders of Israel ask Samuel for a King, he is displeased, and taking it to the Lord in prayer, he receives this answer: "Hearken to the voice of the people in all that they say to you … for they have not rejected you, but they have rejected me from being king over them." [1 Samuel 8:7] Was it not plausible, reading this passage, to think, as Tom Paine would argue, that all monarchy displeased the Lord? Moreover, the Bible, in Genesis, teaches that all men are created in the divine image. And in Acts 10:34 Peter says, "Truly I perceive that God shows no partiality, but in every nation anyone who fears him and does what is right is acceptable to him." Over and over again, the Bible condemns the injustice of rulers who ignore the plight of the powerless—widows, orphans, the poor. To do this, it teaches, is an affront to the God who made mankind and who promises to punish unjust rulers for their crimes. Was it much of a jump to hold, by faith, that all men were equal? Or that they had rights? And that these ideas might lead to changes in the political world?

The colonists were nearly all Christians of one sort or another, and the Bible was the most widely read book in the colonies. Even those who didn't believe the miracles in the Bible (Thomas Jefferson and Ben Franklin are the more famous of these) thought that its moral teaching was the most enlightened ever developed, and consonant with what their minds showed them apart from revelation. Because their local communities recognized these ideas and had endeavored to act in accord with them, the colonists developed a confidence in their ability to make just laws for the whole of America. As King George pushed them outside of his protection, they were willing to dare that, as a people, they could provide for their safety and well-being without him or any king.

Most of us know the words to the Civil War anthem, "The Battle Hymn of the Republic." Fewer know the counterpart of the Revolutionary War. We think it nicely sums up this section.

> Let tyrants shake their iron rod,
> And slavery clang her galling chains,
> We'll fear them not, we trust in God,
> New England's God forever reigns.
> – "CHESTER" The Battle Hymn of the Revolutionary War,
> by William Billings

CHAPTER 3
THE DECLARATION ITSELF

And so, Congress took the fateful step.

Since the next two chapters will analyze the intellectual background and internal structure of the Declaration, we have thought it proper to insert the whole text here. Almost certainly, the reader will have read it before. But a reflective re-reading will be helpful.

The Declaration of Independence of the Thirteen Colonies
In CONGRESS, July 4, 1776
The unanimous Declaration of the thirteen United States of America,

When in the Course of human events, it becomes necessary for one people to dissolve the political bands which have connected them with another, and to assume among the powers of the earth, the separate and equal station to which the Laws of Nature and of Nature's God entitle them, a decent respect to the opinions of mankind requires that they should declare the causes which impel them to the separation.

We hold these truths to be self-evident, that all men are created equal, that they are endowed by their Creator with certain unalienable Rights, that among these are Life, Liberty, and the pursuit of Happiness. That to secure these rights, Governments are instituted among Men, deriving their just powers from the consent of the governed. That whenever any Form of Government becomes destructive of these ends, it is the Right of the People to alter or to abolish it, and to institute new Government, laying its foundation on such principles and organizing its powers in such form, as to them shall seem most likely to effect their Safety and Happiness.

Prudence, indeed, will dictate that Governments long established should not be changed for light and transient causes; and accordingly all experience hath shewn, that mankind are more disposed to suffer, while evils are sufferable, than to right themselves by abolishing the forms to which they are accustomed.

But when a long train of abuses and usurpations, pursuing invariably the same object evinces a design to reduce them under absolute Despotism, it is their right, it is their duty, to throw off such Government, and to provide new Guards for their future security.

Such has been the patient sufferance of these Colonies; and such is now the necessity which constrains them to alter their former Systems of Government. The history of the present King of Great Britain [George III] is a history of repeated injuries and usurpations, all having in direct object the establishment of an absolute Tyranny over these States. To prove this, let Facts be submitted to a candid world.

He has refused his Assent to Laws, the most wholesome and necessary for the public good.

He has forbidden his Governors to pass Laws of immediate and pressing importance, unless suspended in their operation till his Assent should be obtained, and when so suspended, he has utterly neglected to attend to them.

He has refused to pass other Laws for the accommodation of large districts of people, unless those people would relinquish the right of Representation in the Legislature, a right inestimable to them and formidable to tyrants only.

He has called together legislative bodies at places unusual, uncomfortable, and distant from the depository of their public Records, for the sole purpose of fatiguing them into compliance with his measures.

He has dissolved Representative Houses repeatedly, for opposing with manly firmness his invasions on the rights of the people.

He has refused for a long time, after such dissolutions, to cause others to be elected; whereby the Legislative powers, incapable of Annihilation, have returned to the People at large for their exercise; the State remaining in the meantime exposed to all the dangers of invasion from without, and convulsions within.

He has endeavoured to prevent the population of these States; for that purpose obstructing the Laws for Naturalization of Foreigners; refusing to pass others to encourage their migrations hither, and raising the conditions of new Appropriations of Lands.

He has obstructed the Administration of Justice, by refusing his Assent to Laws for establishing Judiciary powers.

He has made Judges dependent on his Will alone, for the tenure of their offices, and the amount and payment of their salaries.

He has erected a multitude of New Offices, and sent hither swarms of Officers to harass our people, and eat out their substance.

He has kept among us, in times of peace, Standing Armies, without the consent of our legislatures.

He has affected to render the Military independent of and superior to the Civil power.

He has combined with others to subject us to a jurisdiction foreign to our constitution and unacknowledged by our laws; giving his Assent to their Acts of pretended Legislation:

For quartering large bodies of armed troops among us:

For protecting them by a mock Trial from punishment for any Murders which they should commit on the Inhabitants of these States:

For cutting off our Trade with all parts of the world:

For imposing Taxes on us without our Consent:

For depriving us in many cases of the benefits of Trial by Jury:

For transporting us beyond Seas to be tried for pretended offences:

For abolishing the free System of English Laws in a neighbouring Province, establishing therein an Arbitrary government, and enlarging its Boundaries so as to render it at once an example and fit instrument for introducing the same absolute rule into these Colonies:

For taking away our Charters, abolishing our most valuable Laws and altering fundamentally the Forms of our Governments:

For suspending our own Legislatures, and declaring themselves invested with power to legislate for us in all cases whatsoever.

He has abdicated Government here by declaring us out of his Protection and waging War against us.

He has plundered our seas, ravaged our Coasts, burnt our towns, and destroyed the lives of our people.

He is at this time transporting large Armies of foreign Mercenaries to complete the works of death, desolation and tyranny, already begun with circumstances of cruelty and perfidy scarcely paralleled in the most barbarous ages, and totally unworthy the Head of a civilized nation.

He has constrained our fellow Citizens taken Captive on the high Seas to bear Arms against their Country, to become the executioners of their friends and Brethren, or to fall themselves by their Hands.

He has excited domestic insurrections amongst us, and has endeavoured to bring on the inhabitants of our frontiers, the merciless Indian Savages, whose known rule of warfare is an undistinguished destruction of all ages, sexes and conditions.

In every stage of these Oppressions We have Petitioned for Redress in the most humble terms. Our repeated Petitions have been answered only by repeated injury. A Prince, whose character is thus marked by every act which may define a Tyrant, is unfit to be the ruler of a free people.

Nor have We been wanting in attentions to our British brethren.

We have warned them from time to time of attempts by their legislature to extend an unwarrantable jurisdiction over us.

We have reminded them of the circumstances of our emigration and settlement here.

We have appealed to their native justice and magnanimity, and we have conjured them by the ties of our common kindred to disavow these usurpations, which would inevitably interrupt our connections and correspondence.

They too have been deaf to the voice of justice and of consanguinity. We must, therefore, acquiesce in the necessity, which denounces our Separation, and hold them, as we hold the rest of mankind, Enemies in War, in Peace Friends.

We, therefore, the Representatives of the United States of America, in General Congress, Assembled, appealing to the Supreme Judge of the world for the rectitude of our intentions, do, in the Name, and by the authority of the good People of these Colonies, solemnly publish and declare.

That these United Colonies are, and of Right ought to be Free and Independent States; that they are Absolved from all Allegiance to the British Crown,

and that all political connection between them and the State of Great Britain is and ought to be totally dissolved;

and that as Free and Independent States, they have full Power to levy War, conclude Peace, contract Alliances, establish Commerce, and to do all other Acts and Things which Independent States may of right do.

And for the support of this Declaration, with a firm reliance on the protection of Divine Providence, we mutually pledge to each other our Lives, our Fortunes, and our sacred Honor.

In 1954, Dumas Malone, a prominent scholar, wrote a book called, *The Story of the Declaration of Independence.* The last chapter of that book is called, "What it Means Now." Malone gave a summary of what he took to be the core of the text. Here it is:

> By birth all men are equal, not in ability or condition, for that has been untrue in all the ages of which we have any record, but in the possession of fundamental rights. Life, liberty, and the pursuit of happiness are mentioned in the great Charter; but more important than any list is the 'truth' that men possess these rights, not because of race or creed or station, but because they are human beings. Here is the eternal answer to bigotry and intolerance of any and every sort.
>
> Government and every other form of public control is a means to human well-being, not an end in itself. Man is not made for the state, but the state for man, and it derives its just powers only from the consent of the governed. In extreme cases, like the one in 1776, this 'truth' justifies political revolution, and in all cases it provides the criterion by which any government or institution should be judged. No sort of rule can justly rest on power alone, and here is the eternal answer to all forms of tyranny over the persons, the property, and the minds of men.

Malone's summary leaves out the list of complaints that explains why the colonists were justified in their revolution, but it effectively presents the Declaration's understanding of government as the servant of man, and its "eternal answer to all forms of tyranny." He omits, however, the references to God. We think this omission is significant, and wrong. To see why, we'll have to unfold the philosophical and religious thought that underlies the text.

CHAPTER 4
THE ROOTS OF AMERICAN LIBERTY

PART 1: The Witness of the Bible

The ideas behind the Declaration were not new with Jefferson. He denied that anything he said was new to the American mind. What he drafted, and Congress amended and adopted in the Declaration, Americans had been thinking for a long time. In this chapter, we will explore some of the sources of these common American opinions.

WRITTEN ON THE HEART

> Then God said, "Let us make man in our image, after our likeness; ... So God created man in his own image, in the image of God he created him; male and female he created them.
> – *Genesis* 1: 26, 27

> For what can be known about God is plain to them, because God has shown it to them....
>
> When Gentiles who have not the law do by nature what the law requires, they are a law to themselves, even though they do not have the law. They show that what the law requires is written on their hearts, while their conscience also bears witness...
> – *Romans* 1:19; 2:14, 15

> We hold these truths to be self-evident, that all men are created equal...
> – *Declaration of Independence*, par. 2

The roots of the Declaration's self-evident truths go back a long way. They are both Biblical and rational, and the Bible itself claims that they are known by reason as well as by faith. The Hebrew Bible teaches in *Genesis* that men, "male and female," are in the divine image. All men. For centuries that was taken by believers, Jewish, Catholic, Orthodox, and Protestant, to mean that our free will and reason are a sharing in the Divine nature; that we are, though decidedly not gods, godlike in our ability to think and act in accordance with our reason.

The reasonable plan for human life, often called the *natural law* or the *law of nature*, is, according to St. Paul, written in our hearts. We know by reason, by the image of God in us, that we are men and that men are not beasts. We know that there are some things that we may do to beasts that we may not do to each other, and that there are others that we must do for each other that we are not obligated to do for the beasts. In other words, we find a ground for both rights and duties in our common humanity, which is a gift of the Creator. As the Declaration assumes, this truth is taught both by reason and faith. The same Bible that proposes it for our belief asserts that it may be known to our minds and is written on our hearts.

These ideas were put in succinct form by President Coolidge in an address in 1924:

> The position which the individual holds in the conception of American institutions is higher than that ever before attained anywhere else on earth. It is acknowledged and proclaimed that he has sovereign powers. It is declared that he is endowed with inalienable rights which no majority, however great, and no power of the Government, however broad, can ever be justified in violating. The principle of equality is recognized. It follows inevitably from belief in the brotherhood of man through the fatherhood of God.
>
> – Calvin Coolidge, *Speech to the Holy Name Society*, Washington, D.C. 1924

Coolidge spoke these words to a Roman Catholic audience. Listen to what he said to a Jewish group the following year:

> I remember to have read somewhere, I think in the writings of the historian Lecky, the observation that 'Hebrew mortar

> cemented the foundations of American democracy.' Lecky had in mind this very influence of the Bible in drawing together the feelings and sympathies of the widely scattered communities.
> – Calvin Coolidge, *Speech at the laying of the cornerstone of the Jewish Community Center*, Washington, May 3, 1925

Later in the speech he added, "Every inheritance of the Jewish people, every teaching of their secular history, and religious experience, draws them powerfully to the side of charity, liberty, and progress."

Coolidge was himself Protestant, a serious and devout Congregationalist. Most of the inhabitants of the colonies before the revolution were Protestants of one sect or another. Coolidge said this of the ministers and other clergy of that time: "The sturdy old divines of those days found the Bible the chief source of illumination for their arguments in support of the patriot cause. They knew the Book."

Those "sturdy old divines" were men convicted both of the liberating truths of the Gospel and of the God-given rights of man. Let's see what they said.

Our first excerpt is taken from an essay by John Wise of Massachusetts. Wise was a Congregationalist, born in Roxbury in 1652. The essay, *A Vindication of the Government of the New England Churches*, was published in 1717. Although the work as a whole is about church government, in particular defending the Congregationalist version of church order, we have chosen a portion on human nature and the natural law or law of nature.

1. The Prime Immunity in Mans State, is that he is most properly the Subject of the Law of Nature. He is the Favourite Animal on Earth; in that this Part of Gods Image, viz. Reason, is Congenial with his Nature, wherein by a Law Immutable, Instamped upon his Frame, God has provided a Rule for Men in all their Actions, obliging each one to the performance of that which is Right, not only as to Justice, but likewise as to all other Moral Virtues, the which is nothing but the Dictate of Right Reason founded in the Soul of Man....
2. The Second Great Immunity of Man is an Original Liberty Instampt upon his Rational Nature. He that intrudes upon this Liberty, Violates the Law of Nature....

3. The Third Capital Immunity belonging to Mans Nature, is an equality amongst Men; Which is not to be denied by the Law of Nature, till Man has Resigned himself with all his Rights for the sake of a Civil State; and then his Personal Liberty and Equality is to be cherished, and preserved to the highest degree, as will consist with all just distinctions amongst Men of Honour, and shall be agreeable with the public Good....

   [and so ...] it would be the greatest absurdity to believe, that Nature actually Invests the Wise with a Sovereignty over the weak; or with a Right of forcing them against their Wills; for that no Sovereignty can be Established, unless some Human Deed, or Covenant Precede: Nor does Natural fitness for Government make a Man presently Governor over another; for that as Ulpian says, by a Natural Right all Men are born free; and Nature having set all Men upon a Level and made them Equals, no Servitude or Subjection can be conceived without Inequality, and this cannot be made without Usurpation or Force in others, or voluntary Compliance in those who Resign their freedom, and give away their degree of Natural Being. And thus we come to consider Man in a Civil State of Being....

   The first Human Subject and Original of Civil Power is the People. For as they have a Power every Man over himself in a Natural State, so upon a Combination they can and do bequeath this Power unto others—and settle it according as their united discretion shall Determine. For that this is very plain, that when the Subject of Sovereign Power is quite Extinct, that Power returns to the People again. And when they are free, they may set up what species of Government they please; or if they rather incline to it, they may subside into a State of Natural Being, if it be plainly for the best....

   – John Wise, from *American Ideas*, ed. Gerald N. Grob and Robert N. Beck, pp 54–61

The next selection is from Samuel West, another New England Congregationalist. West delivered the sermon, from which we quote, to the Council and House of Representatives of Massachusetts, in 1776.

> ... [T]he Deity has also invested us with moral powers and faculties, by which we are enabled to discern the difference

> between right and wrong, truth and falsehood, good and evil; hence the approbation of mind that arises upon doing a good action, and the remorse of conscience which we experience when we counteract the moral sense and do that which is evil. This proves that, in what is commonly called a state of nature, we are the subjects of the divine law and government; that the Deity is our supreme magistrate, who has written his law in our hearts, and will reward or punish us according as we obey or disobey his commands....
>
> ... [t]he authority of a tyrant is of itself null and void; for as no man can have a right to act contrary to the law of nature, it is impossible that any individual, or even the greatest number of men, can confer a right upon another of which they themselves are not possessed; i.e., no body of men can justly and lawfully authorize any person to tyrannize over and enslave his fellow creatures, or do anything contrary to equity and goodness. As magistrates have no authority but what they derive from the people, whenever they act contrary to the common good, and pursue measures destructive of the peace and safety of the community, they forfeit their right to govern the people.
>
> – Samuel West, quoted from *American Political Writing during the Founding Era, Vol. 1*, ed. Charles S. Hyneman, and Donald S. Lutz, pp 411, 416

Next, we offer a short selection from a sermon given in Boston in 1774 with the Royal Governor of Massachusetts, General Thomas Gage, in the audience. Gage had been appointed and given large numbers of redcoats to put down the incipient rebellion in Massachusetts. The preacher, Gad Hitchcock, fearlessly spoke as follows:

> [I]n a state of nature men are equal, exactly on a par in regard to authority; each one is a law to himself, having the law of God, the sole rule of conduct, written on his heart....
>
> No individual has any authority, or right to attempt to exercise any, over the rest of the human species, however he may be supposed to surpass them in wisdom and sagacity....

> And as its [i.e., political power's] origin is from the people, who have not only a right, but are bound in duty, for the preservation of the property and liberty of the whole society, to lodge it in such hands as they judge best qualified to answer to its intention; so when it is misapplied to other purposes, and the public, as it always will, receives damage from the abuse, they have the same original right, grounded on the same fundamental reasons, and are equally bound in duty to resume it, and transfer it to others.
> – Gad Hitchcock, quoted from *American Political Writing during the Founding Era, Vol. 1*, ed. Charles S. Hyneman, and Donald S. Lutz, pp 288–289

Finally, here is an excerpt from a lecture given by a clergyman and educator, the only ordained minister to sign the Declaration, John Witherspoon. Witherspoon served as President of the College of New Jersey, or, as we know it now, Princeton University.

> [R]ights are alienable and unalienable. The first we may, according to justice and prudence, surrender or give up by our own act; the others we may not. A man may give away his own goods, lands, money. There are several things which he cannot give away, as a right over his own knowledge, thoughts, etc. Others which he ought not, as a right to judge for himself in all matters of religion, his right to self-preservation, provision, etc.
> – John Witherspoon, lecture VII, Vol. 3 *Witherspoon's Works*, cited in *American Ideas*, p. 13

SOME REMARKS ON THESE PREACHERS

You must have been struck by the "old-fashioned" language of John Wise. He wrote about two generations before the other preachers we cited, and you can tell something is happening to the way men write, and presumably speak, over that time. It's easy enough to figure out what he means by "instamped," but you won't find that word in a modern novel or newspaper, and you might have to use a large dictionary, or some intelligent guessing, to decide what Wise means by "Immunity." You surely found his capitalization and spelling more archaic than Witherspoon's and the others'. Throughout this book, we will keep the older spelling and punctuation in our original citations, partly because it's simply fun to see it, and partly because we want to notice the changes in language and style that really did happen in the English—or should we say, "American"—language.

Consider the text of Romans 13:1–8 or 1 Peter 2:13–16: "There is no authority except from God...." Did the hearers of these sermons have some reason, from Scripture, to doubt the argument of the colonial preachers? To see how that passage was interpreted as supporting a right of revolution in 1750, one could read the sermon *A Discourse Concerning Unlimited Submission and Non-Resistance to the Higher Powers* by Jonathan Mayhew, delivered in 1750.

President Coolidge, in his great 150th Anniversary speech in honor of the Declaration, claimed that the three central ideas of the Declaration could all be found in John Wise and the other Colonial Preachers. Coolidge identified these ideas as: (1) "the doctrine that all men are created equal; (2) that they are endowed with certain inalienable rights, and; (3) that therefore the source of the just powers of government must be derived from the consent of the governed." Plainly these ideas are in the texts selected above.

A modern reader might be surprised at the explicitly political content of the writings of these clergymen. Such sermons would probably not be well received in certain contemporary quarters. We will return to the role of religious ministers and laypeople in political discourse later.

The more important question is, of course: Are these authors, mostly preachers and teachers, right? Is there a law written on the heart? I, as author of this book would not presume to settle that on *my* authority, though I believe it myself. The two chief witnesses for a "yes" answer are Holy Scripture, for those who believe, and the evidence of each human being's own heart. Do you find such a law within? Who can answer that but you?

CATHOLIC WITNESS: Government by Consent

Though the vast majority of Wise's countrymen were Protestants, it may not be out of place to note the Catholic antecedents of some elements of his thought. Besides the long tradition of reading the passage from *Romans* as pointing to a natural law accessible to human reason, the Declaration principle of governments deriving their authority from the people had been put very forcefully by Cardinal Robert Bellarmine in the 17th Century:

> Note, secondly, that this power [the power of government, or political power] resides ... immediately in the whole state, for this power is by Divine law, but Divine law gives this power to no particular man, therefore, Divine law gives this power to the collected body. Furthermore, in the absence of positive law, there is no good reason why, in a multitude of equals, one rather than another should dominate. Therefore, power belongs to the collected body.
> – Robert Bellarmine, *De Laicis*, Chap. VI

When King James I of England began to assert the contrary of this position, that he ruled by God's appointment, or "divine right," the great Spanish Jesuit, Francisco Suarez, wrote in reply that James' view was, "new and singular, invented to exaggerate the temporal ... power," and that Bellarmine's views were, "the ancient, commonly accepted, and true teaching."

The dates of these Catholic citations are important. There was a bitter quarrel that ran through the 19th century and into the 20th, almost altogether fought on European ground, between "Liberalism" and the Roman Catholic Church. This has led people to think that the Church has been steadily against popular government, contrary to what we quote above from Suarez and Bellarmine. But the truth is that it was the anti-clerical French Revolution, and its intellectual and political heirs in Europe that called forth this anti-democratic reaction from Rome. Before then, things were different. In the Middle Ages, St. Thomas, following Aristotle and also looking to the way Israel was ruled in the Exodus from Egypt, commends a kind of mixed regime. The Catholic clergy of France in 1776 (and in the decades around that year) is sketched by Tocqueville, who researched the matter meticulously, in the following terms:

> They show themselves as hostile to despotism, as favorable to civil liberty, and as eager for political freedom as the Third

> Estate or the nobility. They claim that individual liberty should be safeguarded not by mere promises but by legislation on the lines of the English habeas corpus.... In the political field they proclaimed—and none were more outspoken—the absolute right of all the people to meet together for the purpose of passing laws and freely voting taxes. No Frenchman, they said, should be compelled to pay a tax for which he had not voted in person or through a deputy.... Of 'divine right' *not a word.* [emphasis added]
> – *The Old Regime and the French Revolution*, Part 2, Chapter Eleven

In more recent times, Pope John Paul II spoke as follows, in prepared remarks receiving American ambassador Lindy Boggs at the Vatican:

> The United States carries a weighty and far reaching responsibility, not only for the well being of its own people, but for the development and destiny of people throughout the world.... The Founding Fathers of the United States asserted their claim to freedom and independence on the basis of certain "self-evident" truths about the human person: truths which could be discerned in human nature, built into it by "nature's God."

Thus, they meant to bring into being, not just an independent territory, but a great experiment in what George Washington called "ordered liberty:" an experiment in which men and women would enjoy equality of rights and opportunities in the pursuit of happiness and in service to the common good.

Reading the founding documents of the United States, one has to be impressed by the concept of freedom they enshrine: a freedom designed to enable people to fulfill their duties and responsibilities towards the family and toward the common good of the community. Their authors clearly understood that there could be no happiness without respect and support for the natural groupings through which people exist, develop, and seek the higher purposes of life in concert with others.

The American democratic experiment has been successful in many ways. Millions of people around the world look to the United States as a model, in their search for freedom, dignity, and prosperity. But the continuing success of American democracy depends on the degree to which each new generation, native born and immigrant, makes its own the moral truths on which the Founding Fathers staked the future of their Republic.

Their commitment to building a free society with liberty and justice for all must be constantly renewed if the United States is to fulfill the destiny to which the Founders pledged their "lives ... fortunes ... and sacred honor."

If you think about it, it is only reasonable that readers of a sacred book teaching that all men have dignity in the same way, and from the same Giver, and that all men may be saved by His grace, should find in it the seeds of a political teaching offering political happiness based on the free consent of the equal men who form their own government in accord with His natural law. Of course, these were only seeds until the wonderful year 1776. Our founding fathers made them sprout, and in this work they were aided by other sources, especially the arguments of political thinkers like John Locke, as well as their own experience in self-government. We will turn to the philosophers in the next part of this chapter.

We have argued in this section that the religious sources of the Declaration stretch far into the past, finally to the beginning of the Bible itself. Of course, the scriptural texts need to be read and understood, that is, interpreted. In Colonial America, that interpretation was exemplified by what we read from John Wise and the other preachers. It is by no means the case that all readers of Scripture were in agreement on the principles of civil government then, any more than they are now. But it is not unfair to say, with President Coolidge, that, "in the great outline of its principles, the Declaration was the result of the religious teachings of the preceding period."

PART II: The Witness of the Philosophers

Near the end of his life, Thomas Jefferson wrote to Henry Lee to explain how he came to draft the Declaration:

> When forced, therefore, to resort to arms for redress, an appeal to the tribunal of the world was deemed proper for our justification.

> This was the object of the Declaration of Independence. Not to find out new principles, or new arguments, never before thought of, not merely to say things which had never been said before; but to place before mankind the common sense of the subject, in terms so plain and firm as to command their assent, and to justify ourselves in the independent stand we are compelled to take. Neither aiming at originality of principle or sentiment, nor yet copied from any particular and previous writing, it was intended to be an expression of the American mind, and to give to that expression the proper tone and spirit called for by the occasion. All its authority rests then on the harmonizing sentiments of the day, whether expressed in conversation, in letters, printed essays, or in the elementary books of public right, as Aristotle, Cicero, Locke, Sidney, &c.
> – Jefferson, *Letter to H. Lee*, May 8, 1825

Much of that "harmonizing sentiment," as we have seen above, came from the Bible and the sermons of the day. What about the testimony of reason, especially the witness of the "elementary books of public right?" We will follow Jefferson's own lead in his letter to Henry Lee, and look at some of the ideas that Americans would have borrowed from their philosophical tradition, using the authors Jefferson himself indicated.

ARISTOTLE: Nature and Reason

Aristotle heads the list. He was a student of Plato, a Greek, writing in the fourth century B.C. His writings cover the whole range of human curiosity and wonder, from biology to logic, from the psychology of dreams to the art of poetry, and for our purposes, from Nature (or as he called it, the science of physics) to Politics and Ethics. His practical judgment was so impressive that King Philip II of Macedon gave him the task of tutoring his son and heir. That young student is now known as "Alexander the Great." He profoundly influenced Jewish thought through Moses Maimonides, and Christian thought through the Scholastics. His philosophical work was so masterful that St. Thomas Aquinas, the greatest Scholastic, calls him simply, "the Philosopher," while Dante in his *Divine Comedy,* gives him the title, "the master of those who know." And his works are studied by serious philosophers today. They are of permanent worth.

It is to Aristotle that we owe the idea of 'species' in biology. A species is a kind of creature, marked by a 'specific difference,' which sets it apart from all other plants or animals. Now man is a member of the animal kingdom, similar to other animals in many ways. What is his 'specific difference?' According to Aristotle, (and can a better answer be given even today?) the answer is, 'man is the animal that thinks, the rational animal.'

But in his ethical and political writing, Aristotle went further. He asked a question big with consequence. To what end does man have this ability to think? What had nature in mind for him in giving him this capacity? His answer was that men, by their reason, could find out the way to live and to live well. He held that men live best in a society with other men. So he also defined man as a 'social or political animal.' Here are his exact words, from his book on political theory, called, *Politics*:

> Nature, as we often say, makes nothing in vain, and man is the only animal whom she has endowed with the gift of speech. And whereas mere voice [that is, an animal sound, like a hawk's cry] is but an indication of pleasure and pain, and is therefore to be found in other animals (for their nature attains to the perception of pleasure and pain and the intimation of them to one another, and no further), the power of speech is intended to set forth the expedient and inexpedient, and therefore likewise the just and the unjust. And it is a characteristic of man that he alone has any sense of good and evil, of just and unjust, and the like, and the association of living beings who have this sense makes a family and a political community.
> – Aristotle, *Politics*, Book I, Ch. 2

So one principle from Aristotle is that all men are endowed with a common nature. This common nature allows them to think and speak, and makes them naturally want to live together for their own happiness.

The idea that all classes of men should participate in government also comes from Aristotle. In the 'mixed' form of government the majority, men of ordinary means, and the minority, owners of large properties, check each other's tendency to inflict injustice. He called such a mixed government, 'polity' or 'constitutional government,' and he suggested that it was the best achievable form of political organization. Aristotle considered communist or socialist systems, but rejected them on the sensible grounds that property owned by everyone is cared for by no one. He rejected *absolute* monarchy on the grounds that it would only be just for one man to rule if that man were so superior as to be a god among men, a condition not generally met with in human experience.

Two other principles that Jefferson may have taken from Aristotle are found in the *Ethics,* Aristotle's book on happiness and the good life. One is that there is something "just by nature." That is, justice is not the same thing as whatever men have set up as their laws. The legislator is measured by something not of his own making, something given in the nature of things, especially in human nature.[4] The other idea Jefferson takes from Aristotle is that happiness, the thing at which all men aim, is not pleasure or glory or power, but, "activity of soul in accordance with virtue." He meant by this that the person who lives in accordance with reason and the moral virtues like courage and justice and self-control, which are the highest things in human nature, and who does so with a suitable share of this world's goods throughout his life, is truly happy.[5]

CICERO: Equality and the Natural Law

Cicero was one of the greatest men in the Roman Republic, an orator, philosopher, and statesman, and finally a martyr to the cause of liberty when he was condemned to death by the junta known as the 'Second Triumvirate,' in 43 B.C. Cicero, like Aristotle, taught that there is a higher law that stands above any man-made law, one that lawmakers have a sacred obligation to obey.

> True law is right reason, harmonious with nature, diffused among all, constant, eternal.... It is a sacred obligation not to attempt to legislate in contradiction to this law; nor may it be derogated from nor abrogated. Indeed by neither the Senate nor the people can we be released from this law; nor does it require any but yourself to be its expositor or interpreter. Nor is it one law at Rome and another at Athens; one now and another at a

4 *Ethics*, Book 5, Ch. 7.
5 *Ethics*, Book 1, Ch. 10.

> late time; but one eternal and unchangeable law binding all nations through all time....
> – Cicero, *De Republica*, cited in Lactantius, Div. Inst.

It is striking that Cicero thought that none but oneself need be the interpreter of the natural law. That is because he, like St. Paul a century later, found it written on the human heart, or as Cicero himself would probably have put it, etched in the human mind. Because all men have equal access to the natural law, all men should be equal under that law. Cicero takes the Aristotelian discovery of the common human nature, ascribed to our being rational, and draws from it the Declaration principle of human equality. Thus we find him writing in his *De Legibus* (*On the Laws*):

> There is no one thing so like or equal to one another as in every instance man is to man. And if the corruption of custom and the variation of opinion did not induce an imbecility of minds and turn them aside from the course of nature, no one would more resemble himself than all men would resemble all men. Therefore, whatever definition we give to man will be applicable to the entire human race.
> – Cicero, *De Legibus*, 1

Edwin S. Corwin, a great historian of the Constitution at Princeton University when future U.S. President Woodrow Wilson was head of the University, wrote of the quotation from Cicero above: "... [Equality] is the inescapable consequence of Cicero's notion of the constancy of the distinctive attributes of human nature, those which supply the foundation of natural law." Corwin goes on to say,

> The notion of popular sovereignty, of a social contract, and of a contract between governors and governed are all foreshadowed by Cicero with greater or less distinctness. The notion of a state of nature, on the other hand, is missing, being supplied by Seneca and the early Church Fathers.
> – Edwin S. Corwin, *The 'Higher Law' Background of American Constitutional Law*, pp. 15–16

Jefferson did not mention Seneca to Henry Lee, and he was most likely not widely read in 'the early Church Fathers,' but he did know the work of John Locke, as did most literate and politically aware Americans and Britons of his day.

LOCKE: Natural Right and the State of Nature

John Locke (1632–1704) holds a place among the most important philosophers of the Western Tradition. Like Aristotle, he thought and wrote on ethics, education, physics, and the soul. Locke was friends with the pioneering chemist Robert Boyle, and an avid reader of Rene Descartes and Isaac Newton. Like Aristotle, he played a role in the political life of his day, though where Aristotle was a tutor to a young statesman, Locke was more of an advisor to mature politicians and a civil servant himself. His chief writings are his *Letter on Toleration, Essay Concerning Human Understanding,* and *Two Treatises of Government.* Jefferson no doubt had the *Second Treatise of Government* in mind when he wrote to Lee.

The *Second Treatise* opens with a definition of "political power," its source and its ends. It closes with two chapters on tyranny and the right of rebellion. Political power he defines as "a right of making laws with penalties of death, and consequently all less penalties, for the regulating and preserving of property..." This power implies the legal use of force, and so an executive function, both for domestic order and for protection from "foreign injury." Though he adds that this is "only for the public good," his primary emphasis seems to be on private property.[6]

Where does the right to make laws and use force come from? According to Locke, we must look back to "the state of nature," that is, a real or imagined time before men had any government at all. In this state all men enjoy "perfect freedom to order their actions and dispose of their possessions and persons as they see fit, *within the bounds of the law of nature...*" [italics

6 Is there a tension between Locke's emphasis on property and Aristotle's idea that happiness is found in action in accordance with virtue? Are there virtues that are closely connected to the acquisition and protection of property? What about those virtues that are only remotely related to property, such as chastity, humility, or magnanimity? What is the role of government in fostering any or all of these virtues?

added]. Locke adds that the state of nature is a "state also of equality" echoing Cicero when he remarks that there is "nothing more evident than that creatures of the same species and rank, promiscuously born to the same advantages of nature and the use of the same faculties, should also be equal amongst one another without subordination or subjection...."

Americans can see at once the seeds of what Jefferson would write 100 years later for the Continental Congress: Men are created equal, and there are laws of nature that govern them. Locke takes special pains to insist that the "perfect freedom" of the state of nature does not mean that anyone can do anything:

> The state of nature has a law of nature to govern it ... and reason, which is that law, teaches all mankind who will but consult it that, being all equal and independent, no one ought to harm another in his life, liberty, or possessions....
> – John Locke, *Second Treatise of Government*, Ch. 2

But men are not always observant of the law of nature, or of the dictates of reason generally. Who will enforce the law of nature? In the state of nature, there is no government beyond each individual man. Therefore, the power of the sword, or the executive power, lies in each and every person. Now Locke was a shrewd observer of human behavior. He saw as well as anyone the bias that our natural love of ourselves produces in every human being. So he could not fail to note that leaving the execution of the law to every individual would lead to conflict. A neutral person, a disinterested party, was clearly needed to ensure that justice was done. In short, there was a need for government, or what he had called "political power." But this person is not designated by any obvious signs or marks, nor has God made plain who he is. He is needed, but he is not established by nature. Therefore he and the other magistrates, and ultimately the laws, must be grounded upon the consent of the equal men who form the civil society.

Locke puts the whole argument succinctly in Chapter 8 of the *Second Treatise*:

> Men being, as has been said, by nature all free, equal, and independent, no one can be put out of this estate and subjected to

> the political power of another without his own consent. The only way whereby any one divests himself of his natural liberty and puts on the bonds of civil society is by agreeing with other men to join and unite into a community for their comfortable, safe, and peaceable living one amongst another, in a secure enjoyment of their properties and a greater security against any that are not of it.... When any number of men have so consented to make one community or government, they are thereby presently incorporated and make one body politic wherein the majority have a right to act and conclude the rest.
> – John Locke, *Second Treatise*, Ch.8

Locke was also enough of a realist to anticipate circumstances in which any government, even a republican one, might turn to tyranny. He devoted an entire chapter of the *Second Treatise* to the question of tyranny. In that chapter he remarks:

> It is a mistake to think this fault is proper only to monarchies; other forms of government are liable to it as well as that. For whenever the power that is put in any hands for the government of the people and the preservation of their properties is applied to other ends, and made use of to impoverish, harass, or subdue them to the arbitrary and irregular commands of those that have it, there it presently becomes tyranny, whether those that use it are one or many.
> – John Locke, *Second Treatise*, Ch. 18

Older authors like Plato, Aristotle, and St. Thomas Aquinas describe tyranny as the rule of *one* man not aimed at the common, or public, good. They often go on to say that this happens when a bad man becomes king and puts his desire for wealth or pleasure, for example, over his reason and sense of justice. Locke is explicit in holding that tyranny can be found in a *body* of men who have political power as well as in a monarchy.

Locke is very direct and forceful on what may and should be done when tyranny is being established. First, it is the government's fault, and not the people's. Second, the people shall be the judge of whether it is coming to pass. They need not wait until it has been thoroughly established. Third, the people *should* wait until "a long train of actions show the councils [of the government] all tending that way," i.e., towards tyranny. And fourth, that when this comes to pass, "the people are at liberty to provide for themselves by erecting a new legislative, differing from the other by the change of persons or form, or both, as they shall find it most for their safety and good...."

Locke was sounding a new theme in declaring the right to rebellion. His critics called it a dangerous teaching. Most political thinkers before Locke had been more concerned to discourage men from exercising their right to rebel, if indeed they thought men had such a right at all, than to defend it. Civil war and revolution are terrible things, full of the most extreme sufferings and loss of life and property.

But, replied Locke, there are good reasons to think that a people conscious of its right to rebel will be no more inclined to exercise it than one taught not to. In the first place, it is not abstract principle only, but also the experience of misery that leads men to turn on their masters. The victims of Soviet tyranny, both in Eastern Europe and in the Soviet Empire, were not taught that they had a natural right to rebel, but at length they did. Perhaps if they had cherished such a teaching, and proclaimed it publicly, the very possibility of communist tyranny would not have been so great. Further, from the point of view of the governors, who have no desire to be disgraced, cast from power, and even put to death, their first and best defense against civil war is to govern well.

Locke makes both of these arguments to show that his teaching does not lead to frequent rebellion. He also makes another, in words which are closely followed in the Declaration:

> Great mistakes in the ruling part, many wrong and inconvenient laws, and all the slips of human frailty will be borne by the people without mutiny or murmur. But if a long train of abuses, prevarications, and artifices, all tending the same way, make the design visible to the people, and they cannot but feel what they lie under and see whither they are going, it is not to be wondered that they should rouse themselves and endeavor to put

> the rule into such hands which may secure to them the ends for which government was at first erected...
> – John Locke, *Second Treatise*, Ch. 19, "Of the Dissolution of Government"

ALGERNON SIDNEY: The Whig Martyr

The reputation of the fourth of Jefferson's cited authorities, Algernon Sidney, does not stand so high as the other three, who are in nearly everyone's list of the greats of our civilization. Sidney was a passionate and partisan British Whig, active in Parliament and other government service, who was charged with treason in connection with a conspiracy to assassinate King Charles II (the so-called 'Rye House Plot') and executed in 1683. Sidney's *Discourses Concerning Government*, published in 1698, has been described by Donald Lutz, a 20th century historian, as "especially interesting, since he combines reason and revelation in his analysis, and thus shows how easily the Declaration can be an expression of earlier, biblically based American constitutional thought." Another historian, Bernard Bailyn, says that the American Revolutionary writers "above all ... referred to the doctrines of Algernon Sidney, that 'martyr to civil liberty' whose *Discourses* ... became a textbook of revolution in America."

Two quotations from the *Discourses* may give a taste of Sidney's thought, which is, in most important points, like Locke's:

> Man cannot continue in the perpetual and entire fruition of the Liberty that God hath given him. The Liberty of one is thwarted by that of another; and whilst they are equal, none will yield to any, otherwise than by a general consent. This is the ground of all just governments.

> ... 'tis evident in Scripture God hath ordained Powers; but God hath given them to no particular Person, because by nature all men are equal; therefore he has given Power to the People or multitude.
> – Algernon Sidney, [quoting Bellarmine]

It was Sidney, himself far from being a Catholic, and indeed not obviously of any religious sect of any kind, who cited the Jesuits Bellarmine and Suarez, thus bringing their arguments to a wide English and American audience composed almost entirely of Protestants. And we know that Thomas Jefferson, among others, was paying attention. The Library of Congress owns Jefferson's copy of a book titled *Patriarcha,* by the "Divine Right of Kings" theorist, Robert Filmer. Filmer was an archenemy of the English Whigs, and hence of both Sidney and Locke. Jefferson heavily annotated his copy, marking these sentences, among others. They are Filmer's summary of Bellarmine's ideas:

> Secular or civil power is instituted by man.
>
> It is in the people unless they bestow it upon a prince.
>
> The Divine Law hath given this power to no particular man.
>
> It depends on the consent of the people to ordain over them a king, council, or other magistrates.
>
> If there be lawful cause, the people may change the kingdom into an aristocracy or a democracy.
> – Robert Filmer, *Editorial Comment,* Beatification of Bellarmine, *Catholic World,* May, 1923

The great David Hume, who *is* of the rank of Aristotle, Cicero, and Locke, said of Sidney that he "had maintained principles, favorable indeed to liberty, but such as the best and most dutiful subjects in all ages have been known to embrace; the original contract, the source of power from a consent of the people, the lawfulness of resisting tyrants, the preference of liberty to the government of a single person." If we add to Hume's list the insistence on the natural equality of men as coming from God, together with the law of nature to govern men, we shall have in Sidney's works a concise list of the key propositions Jefferson had recourse to in framing the Declaration.

Jefferson did not tell Lee of all the authors that influenced his and his countrymen's thought in 1776. Surely he could have mentioned William Blackstone, the great English jurist, and the French political philosopher, Charles Montesquieu; the former for the natural law, the latter for the excellence of 'mixed government' and the separation of powers. Plutarch, Livy, and other authors from classical antiquity were part of the story, too. And of course, the Bible. The key point is that our founders saw these authors, both philosophical and sacred, as pointing to a common teaching, of human rights and natural law, of the dignity of man and of the political life, and of the possibility of just, free, republican government, based upon the consent of the governed. And with this in mind they made their Declaration, their revolution, and us.

CHAPTER 5
THINKING THROUGH THE DECLARATION

In this chapter, we will look carefully at the details and language of the Declaration. We will assume that the Congress, the drafters, and the signers made *sense*. They knew what they wanted to declare, and they did so with precision. After all, if men are capable of ruling themselves by reason, they must also be able to communicate their thoughts clearly to one another so that what each thinks can become known to the other. We will not submit to the "tyranny of relativism." This means that we will be paying attention to particular words and arguments in hopes of seeing the truth, and that we will not say, as many do, that one thing is true "for me" and another "for you."

INDEPENDENCE

Let's start at the beginning, with the first paragraph.

> When in the course of human events, it becomes necessary for one people to dissolve the political bands....

We note in the first place that Congress is arguing for separation. The resulting war was called the War of Independence, and July 4th is called "Independence Day." America was separating from Great Britain. This meant that we would no longer form one political society with what they later call, "our British brethren." It meant that we would become independent.

The founders held that this separation was "necessary," and that they were compelled to it by causes outside themselves. "Necessary" here does not mean that "there was nothing they could do about it," as, for example, it *must be* that a part is always less than the whole, or that when a triangle is right angled, then the square on the hypotenuse is equal to the squares on the other two sides, or that water *must* flow downhill.

The necessity that they had in mind was *moral* necessity. When a young man says, "I *had to* answer my country's call," or a witness admits, "I was *compelled* to say what I knew about the charges," he or she is acknowledging the force of moral necessity. Perhaps I would much rather stay home with my family or at work or school. Perhaps I grieve that my testimony will convict a friend or relative. Nonetheless, I must do it. It is a duty. I may be reluctant, but I must do what is right.

Congress was indeed reluctant to separate from "our British brethren." Ties of blood—"consanguinity … ties of our common kindred"—are cited in the concluding paragraphs of the Declaration. But, that same passage goes on to say, "We must, therefore, acquiesce in the *necessity* which denounces our separation…." Their claim, consequently, was that the separation from the British government, and hence the British people, was their duty.

Moreover, since separation, or dissolving political bands, sometimes called "rebelling,"is generally and reasonably held to be a dangerous if not desperate action, they also felt a duty to explain their reasons. And not only to the British, but to "the opinions of mankind." They called this duty a "decent respect."

The word "decent" is noteworthy. A decent person feels himself measured by a standard. He is also capable of feeling shame for his words and deeds, should they fall short of that standard. He cares about what others think of him. A decent respect for the opinions of others implies that the others, too, are decent, or capable of decency, and hence have dignity. These "others" are all our fellow human beings.

Thus the founders bore witness to that common human dignity which would ground their own independence. That dignity has a source, namely the "laws of nature and of nature's God."

We have seen in previous chapters that they drew their belief in, and their knowledge of those laws from Scripture and from the arguments of such men as John Wise and John Locke, and from the testimony of their own hearts. But this source of our common dignity has another consequence. If men have the power and right of separation because they are "made in the image and likeness of God," then when they have good reason, genuine *moral necessity*, they may also form a new people and take their stand among "the powers of the earth." That is, they may form a new political community by the right invested in them by their Creator.

REVOLUTION

The second paragraph moves from our right of separation to unalienable rights, and next onto our hopes for a new order of government. It gives the general reasons that would justify revolution. To *assert* a right does not make its *exercise* right. I may have a right to free speech, but that doesn't mean I should, by speaking, betray a confidence, slander my fellow man, or inform on a fellow citizen.

The Declaration spells out what God and nature have given us in terms of unalienable rights. "Unalienable" means not *able* to be given away. The first of these unalienable rights is the right to life. Because God has made us, we cannot rightly destroy our lives, His workmanship. Next, because He has made us reasonable and equal, we cannot give away our liberty to use that reason in living well and in aiming at our happiness. These, then, are the unalienable rights that the declaration says governments are to secure: Life, Liberty, and the Pursuit of Happiness.

"Pursuit of happiness" was consciously chosen by Jefferson and the Congress to be inserted in place of "property,"which was the term found after liberty in Locke's *Second Treatise*. There are two good reasons for this change. One, there is no unalienable right to *property* in the ordinary sense of the word. Property rights are precisely "alienated" every time we freely sell or buy something. Better would be a right to *acquire* property, by labor or other honest means. This indeed could be fundamental and inalienable, because it is grounded in our human nature.

When George Mason drafted the Virginia Declaration of Rights, he acknowledged the force of this reasoning by including among the "inherent rights" of man "the means of acquiring and possessing property." But by speaking of a right to "acquire," we would be already in the realm of "pursuits." This leads us to the second reason.

We pursue other things than property, often at the expense of property. Is property, especially in the sense of items able to be bought and sold, the sum total of the things that we think are ours, or for which we labor? Surely not. For example, we will spend money to defend our reputation, to please a friend, to help the poor, to learn a skill, to acquire knowledge, to honor God. We are happy if we succeed. The more inclusive and nobler term, "happiness," and not happiness itself, but the pursuit of it, was the founders' choice. It was a wise one.

Since governments exist by human consent to secure these rights, if any government becomes destructive of them, the people may and, if possible, should, rebel. What then? If the rebellion succeeds, they may and should form a new government better than the tyrannical one they have abolished. What will make it better? How shall the new government be judged?

The answer to the first question can be as simple as a change of the persons who rule. Get the old king out and replace him with a new one. Or it could be as complex as forming new structures of government and society. Let us call this complex answer, "Political Revolution." Political revolutions have a nasty habit of turning into purges, with the new regime often no better, or even worse, than the old one. The boldness of the Declaration may be seen in its avowal of the possibility of a political revolution. The colonists declared that they had the right to "alter or abolish" the *form* of government, and to lay the foundations for a *new* government, "on such principles, and organizing its powers in such form as to them shall seem most likely to effect their safety and happiness." This gives us the grounds for judging the new government. Is it likely to insure safety and promote happiness?

Of course, the Declaration was primarily concerned with independence. Although it gave the principles on the basis of which Americans would erect their fundamental laws, it set up no *structure* of government. The Congress that adopted it was a kind of emergency "committee of the whole" for the American people, but the Declaration itself does not propose articles of confederation or a constitution. In looking to the Declaration for such a structure, we must be content with the spirit, not the letter, of constitutional law. We can see a most important part of that spirit in the part of the Declaration that we are now analyzing.

John Locke's theory emphasized government's role in protecting individual rights against injustice, primarily a negative function, while neglecting its positive role in attaining good things. In other words, he is strong on rights, but weak on ends, especially virtue and the good life, as that life transcends the acquisition of property. To this day Americans find it easier to discover and fight for rights than to praise virtues and proclaim duties.

The most famous early flag of the revolution had a rattlesnake stitched over the thirteen stripes and the words, "Don't Tread on Me." We were, and are, jealous for our rights. This can lead to unending squabbling, with each person trying to get his own rights and not noticing he is treading on others. And even consulting our rights with due concern for others doesn't say much about what we are to do with our lives, liberties, and property once we have recognized or secured them.

The older political theory, inherited from the Greek and Roman thinkers and from our religious heritage, looked to ends. "Respice finem," wrote old Cicero. Laws were for the sake of virtue and finally, blessedness or happiness, i.e., that men might live well. Americans at the time of the Revolution stayed true to this ancient view in many instances. Witness the following language in the Constitution of Pennsylvania, adopted in 1776:

> ... a frequent recurrence to fundamental principles, and a firm adherence to justice, moderation, temperance, industry, and frugality are absolutely necessary to preserve the blessings of liberty, and keep a government free.

And this, from Virginia's Constitution:

> That no free government, or the blessings of liberty, can be preserved to any people, but by a firm adherence to justice, moderation, temperance, frugality, and virtue, and by frequent recurrence to fundamental principles.

It is to the credit of the founders that they point us in this direction in the Declaration. They do it by speaking of the rights listed earlier as the "ends" of government, and by replacing "pursuit of happiness" — a *right*— with happiness itself, an *end*. It is, we may securely state, self-evident that happiness is not a right. Men can and must pursue it, and they have a right to, but the degree to which they achieve it will depend on many things *not* in their power. It will also depend on one very great thing that largely is in their power, especially in a democratic republic: Good government.

PRUDENCE

> Prudence, indeed, will dictate that governments long established should not be changed for light and transient causes...

What is prudence? Why does the Declaration consider its dictates before making its list of charges against the king and finally declaring independence?

In order to act well, men, as reasonable creatures, must also think well. Thinking well about what is to be done goes by the name of "practical wisdom" or "prudence." It includes a sense for what is good and right, and an ability to choose the best ways to accomplish it. Sometimes it means patiently waiting and *not* acting, because there is no decent or safe way to achieve what would otherwise be desirable.

In our Western Tradition, practical wisdom is often called simply "wisdom," and both the Greek philosophers and the Hebrew Bible praise the wisdom that directs the community as higher than the wisdom of a private man. Political prudence they call almost 'god-like.' The man who has it, and who has power, is the statesman.

There is an obvious reason for those who were about to take the bold step of separating and even revolutionizing to pause and give wisdom her due. Passions were high; blood had been shed; the arrogance of the King was plain to the colonists in the spectacle of Boston occupied by redcoats, no stirring of sails in its harbor; Falmouth in the North and Norfolk in the South burning.

But passion is not always a wise counselor. This revolution was to be deliberate, as coolly determined upon as possible, in part because it was being made in the name of the capacity of the people to govern itself. It was essential that the Declaration be, and be seen to be, the work, not of a mob, but of an assembly of rational men reasoning together.

Prudence makes revolution more difficult. It is not enough for the patriots to show their rights are less secure than they would wish. They must prove that the King shows in his words and deeds a tendency that makes the act of revolution not only the right of the colonists but also their duty. These words and deeds will be published and the tendency explained in the list of grievances that follows, but the list makes for dry reading compared to the great general ideas of the first two paragraphs of the Declaration. To read it with understanding requires that you be something of a lawyer and a historian now, perhaps a journalist or regular reader of newspapers then. You might even say that it requires a share of statesmanship.

A WORD ON WORDS

Some of the words used in the Declaration are uncommon, or used in a sense uncommon in today's English. "Unalienable," for instance. A bit of dictionary work may be in order for contemporary readers.

When considering a word, attention to the roots of the term may give good evidence for its significance. For example, "democracy" comes from two Greek words, one for the people, *demos*, and one for ruling, or mastering, *kratein.* Another good way to get the sense of a word in Jefferson's time is to check out how it is used in a familiar text, like Shakespeare or above all the King James Bible. Try this with "happiness." You might start with Psalm 144:15.

A LONG TRAIN OF ABUSES: Tyranny, the Branches of Government, and the Seeds of a Constitution

The longest and central part of the Declaration is our next object of study. In it the founders give the reasons that impelled them to independence and indicate some of the considerations that should direct the formation of the new government. There are twenty-eight specific complaints against the English King, followed by a conclusion that the king is a tyrant, and his government deaf to the colonists' pleas, and accordingly, the separation is necessary.

The first seven all include the term, "laws," or in the case of the fourth and fifth, "representative houses," and "legislative power," i.e., the bodies and authority by which laws are made. You might think that the grounds for revolution or independence would normally be that the People suffers under bad laws. Look carefully at these seven complaints. All of them have to do with blocking the passage of laws aimed at "the public good." The fifth charge against the King is especially noteworthy. The law making power is there said to be "incapable of annihilation." The thought is that men are entitled to government by God and nature, and that the power to make laws is delegated to the legislative body. When the action or even the existence of that body are impaired, the power returns to its origin, the People. Law making is so fundamental to humanity that the authority to make law *cannot* be destroyed.

From law making the list moves on to judging. Here, too, the charge is not that the king imposed bad judges, but that he refused the People its fundamental right to *have* judges, and to have them be independent. In particular, judges must be free from pressure from the executive, but the king has made them "dependent on his will alone...."

We begin to see in this list of charges the outlines of the branches of government that will be established in the American Constitution. The king is said to have blocked the exercise of the legislative and judicial branches, and to have interfered with the independence of the judicial. He has usurped powers that ought to be exercised by others.

A little more than a decade later, Publius will say of such usurpation:

> The accumulation of all powers, legislative, executive, and judiciary, in the same hands, whether of a one, a few, or many, and whether hereditary, self-appointed, or elective, may justly be pronounced the very definition of tyranny.
> – *Federalist 47*

All the remaining charges, numbers 10–28, are about things the King is said to have *done*. That is, they are abuses of the executive power. Note how many of them have to do with military policy, the first responsibility of the executive in the Constitution. Some concern excessive cost and inconvenience of the military forces, or of taxes and what we would now call bureaucrats. One of particular relevance today is that population increase is a desirable thing. An obvious one is that the civil authority should keep the peace and protect the lives of the citizens. Others involve executive suspension of the powers of the other two branches, partially repeating what was set out in the first nine complaints.

The last charge refers to British offers of liberty to slaves, should they run away and serve the King's forces. This complaint is taken as a stain on the honor of the Declaration. We will return to slavery and the Declaration later.

Anyone who complains about something must have in mind the opposite state of affairs, a good and just one, to serve as a standard. When it comes to the complaints of the Declaration, that standard is evidently one in which the structure of government respects the different functions and lines of division between the branches. When our ancestors came to erect such a structure, first in the Articles of Confederation, and next in the Constitution, they took their bearings in large measure from the principles laid down in the Declaration. They had outlined the features of tyranny in King George, and they acted to prevent tyranny for themselves and us in the Constitution. That is why they said, in the preamble to the Constitution, that the People was acting, "[to] secure the blessings of liberty to ourselves and our posterity."

WORDS OF POWER, AND THE POWER BEHIND THE WORDS

After the deep principles of the opening section and the painful details of the central part, the close comes with a sense of solemn necessity. Here,

> the representatives of the UNITED STATES OF AMERICA," acting "in the name of the good people of these colonies … declare That these United Colonies are, and of right ought to be, FREE and INDEPENDENT STATES;

They knew, of course, that this meant war with Britain, and that no one could be sure who would win that war, or whether any of them would survive it with his life or liberty. They were sure that, as representatives of the people, of the *good* people of the colonies, they had the right and the duty to declare independence, and that their declaration made it a *fact.*

Much earlier in this book, we compared the Declaration to a marriage. This is where that comparison is most plain. You are married when you say, "I do." We became independent when we *said* we were, after due deliberation and decent notification of mankind. That is why we celebrate the Fourth of July, and it is also probably why the new name, "United States of America," was printed in the original all in capital letters.

Another way of saying this is that genuine declarations are a special kind of language, like vows or contracts. They not only express our thoughts or desires, as when we say "It's warm today," or "I'd like a sandwich." They make what they say real, as in a marriage vow. They are words of power, almost like the creative words in *Genesis* that God spoke, "and it was so." The Declaration says that the colonies "*are*, and of right ought to be, free," that "all political connection between them and the state of Great Britain *is*, and ought to be, totally dissolved." It says that "as FREE and INDEPENDENT

STATES, [we] have full power to levy war, conclude peace, contract alliances, establish commerce, and to do all other things which INDEPENDENT STATES may of right do."

Congress declared these things conscious of the people's power to have them so. But it did not think might makes right. The colonies ... "are, and *of right ought to be*, FREE and INDEPENDENT...." The tie to Britain "is and *ought to be,* totally dissolved."

And most important, Congress appealed "to the Supreme Judge of the world for the rectitude of our intentions...." It was His law that entitled us to independence in the opening of the Declaration. It is His judgment (and not that of men to which we owe, indeed, a decent respect) by which we would be judged. And it is His supervising power, "DIVINE PROVIDENCE," upon which our founders relied in the war that all expected would follow their declaration.

War would come. The signers knew it; some would in fact lose their property or their lives in the revolution. That they were willing to take the risk is a sign that, though government may be founded on rights to things we desire, like life and property, men living the political life keep an eye on something higher. Life itself, Aristotle taught long ago, is for the sake of the *good* life, and a noble man will risk many material goods for his honor, the sign of a life well lived. The founders thought it was an honor, even a sacred thing, to share in a common struggle for liberty, and so they closed the Declaration with those two words: "sacred honor."

HONOR AND POLITICS

In a certain way, it was easier for the founders to see that they were serving in a high cause, an honorable one, in the revolution, than it is for us to see that we are doing something similar in performing our civic duty today. More seems to be demanded of a man to stand up to a line of British Grenadiers than to decide rightly on a school bond issue, or to obey the zoning laws of his county.

It was not the risk alone, or the fact that battles would ensue that gave the founding its noble or honorable character. Politics itself, rightly pursued, is honorable. The Ancient Romans used to call the public life "*cursus honorum*" the path of honors. The following quotations, from Alexander Hamilton, David Ramsay (a member of the Continental Congress who also wrote a history of the Revolution), and Abraham Lincoln, illustrate the extent to which the founding of America elevated men's thoughts and kindled in their hearts a noble love of fame and virtue.

> ... [a member of Congress] is to be regarded not only as a legislator, but as the founder of an empire. A man of virtue and ability, dignified with so precious a trust, would rejoice that fortune had given him birth at a time, and placed him in circumstances so favorable for promoting human happiness. He would esteem it not more the duty, than the privilege and ornament of his office, to do good to mankind; from this commanding eminence, he would look down with contempt upon every mean or interested pursuit.
> – Alexander Hamilton, *Publius Letter III*, November 16, 1778

> In the years 1775 and 1776, the country, being suddenly thrown into a situation that needed the ability of all its sons, these generally took their places, each according to the bent of his inclination. As they generally pursued their objects with ardor, a vast expansion of the human mind speedily followed.... It seemed as if the war not only required, but created talents. Men whose minds were warmed with the love of liberty, and whose abilities were improved by daily exercise, and sharpened with a laudable ambition to serve their distressed country, spoke, wrote, and acted, with an energy far surpassing all expectations which could be reasonably founded on their previous acquirements.
> – David Ramsay, *The History of the American Revolution*, 1793

> Then, all that sought celebrity and fame, and distinction expected to find them in the success of that experiment. Their all was staked upon it—their destiny was inseparably linked with it. Their ambition aspired to display before an admiring world a practical demonstration of the truth of a proposition, which had hitherto been considered, at best not better, than problematical; namely, the capacity of a people to govern themselves. If they succeeded, they were to be immortalized; their names were

> to be transferred to counties and cities, and rivers and mountains; and to be revered and sung, and toasted through all time. If they failed, they were to be called knaves and fools, and fanatics for a fleeting hour; then to sink and be forgotten. They succeeded. The experiment is successful; and thousands have won their deathless names in making it so.
> – Abraham Lincoln, *Address before the Young Men's Lyceum of Springfield*, Illinois, January 27, 1838

Hamilton, Ramsay, and Lincoln point us towards the conclusion we have been arguing for in this entire chapter: the Declaration opens a way to a political life not only based on the rational capacity of mankind, but ending in high and noble political action. We will show later that Americans have risen to this challenge by returning to the principles of the Declaration in times of crisis. What of our own times?

CHAPTER 6
AMERICAN CONSTITUTIONS

PART ONE: THE ARTICLES OF CONFEDERATION

> ... That whenever any Form of Government becomes destructive of these ends, it is the Right of the People to alter or to abolish it, and to institute new Government, laying its foundation on such principles and organizing its powers in such form, as to them shall seem most likely to effect their Safety and Happiness.
> – *Declaration of Independence*

Through the Declaration of Independence, the united colonies had abolished their old form of government under the king. But they also had to institute a new government that would bring about their safety and happiness in a manner consistent with the principles of the Declaration. Although separation was the more momentous and daring, forming a new government was necessarily much more laborious.

As noted in the next sentence in the Declaration, the founders were well aware of the difficulty of this labor. Perhaps the new form would fail even more miserably than the old. But actions of king and Parliament had forced them to try and see whether they could not do better. The Continental Congress had already acted to establish the new government before they had officially declared their old one defunct. At the same time they authorized Jefferson to draft the Declaration, they also established a committee to draft articles that would establish the form of government. Within a few days of the acceptance of the Declaration, Congress was presented with a draft of what were called "Articles of Confederation." Because of the difficulties of the matter and the press of the war, which Congress had to oversee, it was over a year before they accepted the articles and presented them to the states.

Most of the state legislatures ratified the articles within a year, by the end of 1778, though only in 1781 did the last state agree to them.

The Articles of Confederation and the state constitutions that were developed in the same period represented the first stage in the great experiment of republican government. Nothing like them had ever been attempted before. Written constitutions that detailed what a government could and could not do, how it must go about its business, who should do what, had hardly ever been attempted outside of America, and never to the extent that the Americans now proposed. Most societies of men had worked according to custom or laws that arose from particular situations or conflicts. To sit down, discuss, and then deliberately decide what manner of government would most likely bring about safety and happiness was rare. To do this in the name of the people, and then to submit the result to them for their approval, was radical.

Americans, however, had already had more experience at constitution making than anyone else in history. From the time of the first settlers, Americans in small groups had been compacting with each other to form societies, and then forming governments to rule over them. They had experience with what worked and didn't work. They even had experience of confederation, that is, of joining smaller societies together to achieve better the ends of government.

Even with all this experience, however, their many failures made them feel how difficult their project was. The fifteen-year period from 1776 to 1791 saw states propose constitutions once, twice, even three times, as they discovered fundamental flaws in the governments that arose. Given the difficulty, it is amazing that in the most novel of their experiments, a united government for all the states, only two attempts produced the wonder that is our Constitution.[7]

In the present chapter, we will look closely at both attempts, the Articles of Confederation and the Constitution, to see what made them fitting forms of government for a people committed to Declaration principles. Besides this text, the reader should have and consult the two constitutional documents as he reads what follows.

7 Donald Lutz's book, *The Origins of American Constitutionalism,* explores in detail the history of confederation and constitutional government in America. A fine account of these matters, with special emphasis on the state constitutions, may be found in Morrison's *Oxford History of the American People,* 1965 ed., pp. 270–281.

THE ARTICLES OF CONFEDERATION

Probably the most striking aspect of the Articles, especially for those who are familiar with the Constitution, can be summed up in the word "confederation." What exactly does that mean? Article Two indicates that states remain independent; Article Three describes confederation as "a firm league of friendship." Are the states forming, not one government, but an alliance like NATO?

The immediate answer to the latter question is, no. By means of the Declaration of Independence, the Americans, through their representatives, had asserted their independence as "a People", not "Peoples;" they declared the independence of the "united Colonies," not simply of the colonies. By declaring their independence commonly, through a common body, the Continental Congress, and a common document, the Declaration, the Americans also formed themselves as a People.

This fact is abundantly confirmed in the Articles. The Articles were proposed by Congress to the states in 1777, which is called "the Second Year of the Independence of America," and it was essentially ratified "in the third year of the independence of America." In these words, the Articles recognize that "America" was formed as a People by their decision to make their declaration of independence a common act. The official title of the document is "Articles of Confederation and perpetual Union between" the thirteen states. The last article, Article XIII, forcefully claims that the states must abide by all the decisions made according to the Articles by the common Congress of the states. It then adds with great significance, "and the Union shall be perpetual." However much or little the independent states committed to their common government, they committed to it forever. They had already determined that their safety and happiness, their ties of blood, language, culture and ideals, should make them a People, and they meant to abide by that act forever.

As an act of perpetual Union, the Articles differ essentially from any treaty or compact between fully independent nations. Alliances and leagues are usually established for limited, renewable terms. Decisions made according to them must be confirmed by the proper governing power of each state, which may at any time decide to withdraw from the league. Under the Articles, the United States bound themselves in perpetuity to a form of government that could only be altered by the United States in Congress, with the concurrence of every state. A single state could not alter or abolish the government on its own.

The intention to form a government suited to a united People is found particularly in Article IV, according to which a "free inhabitant" of any state shares fully in the "privileges and immunities of free citizens" whenever he is in any other state. No American would be prevented from relocating anywhere in the United States. Any contract that he had formed in one state would be recognized by all the other states. This act would "secure and perpetuate mutual friendship and intercourse among the people of the different States of the Union...." It would solidify their sense of themselves as a People, as Americans. It was this sense of unity as a People that, more than anything else, would ensure the perpetual existence of the new nation.

Why, then, the strong emphasis on the independence and sovereignty of the states? As was mentioned earlier, for Americans, deliberately forming governments was not a new enterprise. During the first century of colonization, a multitude of new civil and church governments were formed by groups of colonists. The process was different in places, but it occurred everywhere. This process often involved confederation, especially in the New England colonies.

New England was settled by small groups of pious, like-minded, and resolute men and women. When they arrived, they quickly formed themselves into a community under a common compact and government. A number of towns were started in different areas, which began and for a time remained independent of each other. It wasn't long, however, before the inhabitants of these towns realized that many benefits were to be gained from joining together.

While they valued their independence, and didn't always entirely like or agree with the views of the men in neighboring towns, they understood that they were unable to secure certain important aspects of their "safety and happiness" alone. So they formed a new compact, a larger society. In this way, the united colonies of Massachusetts, Connecticut, and the "Rhode Island and Providence Plantations" were formed.

In forming these larger societies, the townspeople did not abandon their town governments. While realizing that certain important ends could only be obtained by uniting with other towns, they also believed that their town communities were adequate for most of the purposes of daily life. They thought a united government would serve a few definite tasks well, but not most of the tasks of government. So they deliberately limited the authority of the new governments, retaining most powers and duties for the smaller town governments.

The Americans brought this same notion of limited confederations to the formation of a national government. Although the colonies had led mostly separate lives for their first 150 years, the crisis with Britain had quickly convinced them of the need to be and remain united. Certain crucial aspects of their safety and happiness depended on their perpetual union. But by no means all. Just as they were content with town or other local governments for most of the affairs of life, so they were content with their colonial or state governments for most of the functions that they had fulfilled up to that time. So the union was to be a federation, with the national government strictly limited with regard to what it would be responsible for doing. Article II makes this abundantly clear by retaining to the states their complete independence in matters not expressly assigned to the united government.

What were the matters more competently addressed by the United States than by the states separately? It is striking that the powers given to the United States in the Articles are those very acts that the Declaration explicitly states to be indicative of independent nations. In its last paragraph, having dissolved the bonds joining them to the British crown and people, the Declaration claims for the united colonies, that:

> … as Free and Independent States, they have Full Power to levy War, conclude Peace, contract Alliances, establish Commerce, and to do all other Acts and Things which Independent States may of right do.

These acts all have in common that they occur between societies of peoples that are not one, and consequently do not submit to common government. Because of this, they must regulate their affairs, not according to laws established by a common government, but according to agreements: peace treaties, defensive alliances, trade agreements. The authority to enter into such agreements or to declare war if necessary is expressly given to the

Congress of the United States (Article IX) and is expressly denied to the states (Article VI). Single states are not to act as "Free and Independent States" either with respect to foreign nations like France, nor with respect to each other. They cannot enter into compacts among themselves without the consent of the United States. Their right to maintain a standing army is limited. Their coinage, the means of commerce, is subject to the determination of the Congress. States must submit disputes with other states to the federal government.

Although the Articles bound together the people of America in one government they finally proved inadequate to the task. A detailed account of these inadequacies may be found in *Federalist Papers* numbers 15–23. While giving to the federal government the ends appropriate to it, the states feared to give it powers adequate to achieve those ends. The federal government could apportion taxes, but could not collect them. That was left up to the states. It could regulate coinage, but had no power to enforce its regulations. It could negotiate treaties with other nations, but could not compel states and individuals to live up to them. It had no courts to judge violators of its laws. It was difficult for it to come to *any* decision. In matters of any importance, the consent of nine states, each with a single vote, was needed to act. Given the diversity of the states, such agreement was all too often impossible. Yet the Articles, for all their weaknesses, were an important first attempt at forming a government consistent with the Declaration.

PART TWO: THE CONSTITUTION

> ... the American Constitution is, so far as I can see, the most wonderful work ever struck off at a given time by the brain and purpose of man.
> – W.E. Gladstone, Prime Minister of Great Britain, Sept, 1878

The Constitution of the United States is unique in the history of the world, the providential product of a group of outstanding statesman, who in themselves contained the genius of a great people and of the Western political experience of 2000 years. It has lasted for over two centuries, and is still admired and drawn on by statesmen around the world for its wisdom. This chapter on the Constitution does not pretend to plumb its depths. Many books have been written on the subject, a number of which are referenced in the back of this book for those who want to understand it better.

What we want to accomplish here is to fulfill something of the promise we made in the beginning of the book, where it was claimed that, as the Law of Moses can't be understood apart from the covenant of Abraham, which is its spirit, so the Constitution is only properly understood in the light of the principles laid down in the Declaration. Considered in itself, the Constitution appears to be something of a mechanical or technical manual. "How to elect Representatives; how to elect Senators; how to admit new states; Congress can do certain enumerated things; it cannot do other things;" and so on. But the Constitution doesn't stand by itself; it comes after and presupposes the Declaration, as we hope to show.

THE PREAMBLE

The Constitution begins with a short paragraph, or long sentence, as famous as the opening paragraphs of the Declaration. "We the People of the United States.... " This paragraph is known as the "Preamble." A quick reading breaks it into three parts, explaining Who is doing What and Why. The second of these parts, the "in order to" section, is the longest, consisting of six separate goals to be attained by the Constitution.

Why did the framers of the Constitution bother to enumerate these goals? Before we look at each particular goal, let us note something fundamental: Just as the founders had a duty to explain to themselves and to the world the reason why they were separating from England, so they had a duty to explain to themselves and others exactly why they were giving the national government the particular structure detailed in the following articles.

As we have seen, the founders understood the importance of prudence. In any venture, the prudent man looks to clearly understood goals. These goals make sense of all the choices he makes on his way to attaining them. They also prevent him, as long as he keeps them clearly in mind, from making serious mistakes. A doctor has to keep clearly in mind his goal of helping the patient recover. He cannot rely simply on the procedures he learned in medical school, because they might fail in any particular case. A standard procedure applied to a particular patient may be harmful and not helpful. The measure is not the procedure, but health.

Political decisions, judgments and interpretations are even less subject to mindless, automatic procedure. In order to use the Constitution effectively, its framers realized that legislators, officers, and judges would have to keep in mind the goals for which it was intended. The Preamble is their attempt to express its goals in as concise a formula as possible. As one early influential commentator on the Constitution wrote:

> [The Preamble's] true office is to expound the nature and extent and application of the powers actually conferred by the Constitution, and not substantively to create them.
> – Joseph Story, 1833

In this section, we will look at the ends stated in the Preamble.

IN ORDER TO FORM A MORE PERFECT UNION

> ... Whereas experience hath evinced that there are defects in the present Confederation.... Resolved that in the opinion of Congress it is expedient that on the second Monday in May next a Convention of delegates who shall have been appointed by the several states be held at Philadelphia for the sole and express purpose of revising the Articles of Confederation and reporting to Congress and the several legislatures such alterations and provisions therein as shall ... render the federal constitution adequate to the exigencies of Government and the preservation of our Union.
> – Resolution of Congress, Feb. 21, 1787

By February 1787, it had become abundantly clear that the Congress established under the Articles of Confederation was failing as governing body. In the resolution calling for a convention to revise the Articles, Congress implied what was in fact the case: The continued existence of the Union was in danger, because the constitution (the Articles) was inadequate to the needs ("exigencies") of the national Government.

The problem was not to be found primarily in the role assigned to it under the Articles, but in the means to perform its assigned tasks effectively.

While desiring to live under one government, the states had feared to entrust adequate power to that government. Having just rid themselves of one tyrant and tyrannical legislature in King George and Parliament, they did not want to run the risk of having another closer to home. In his letter presenting the proposed Constitution to Congress, George Washington, President of the Convention, recognizes this fear as the source of the difficulties.

> The friends of our country have long seen and desired, that the power of making war, peace, and treaties, of levying money and regulating commerce, and the correspondent executive and judicial authorities should be fully and effectually vested in the general government of the Union; but the impropriety of delegating such extensive trust to one body of men is evident—hence results the necessity of a different organization.
>
> – George Washington, Letter of Transmittal, Sept. 17th, 1787

In the beginning of this sentence, Washington enumerates the powers that should belong to a general government. He includes the four mentioned in the Declaration, and adds that of taxation or "levying money." As we saw, all of these powers were assigned by the Articles to the general government, although the power of taxation consisted simply in a levy against the states.

The difficulties are suggested in the next few phrases. The Articles did not provide a means of enforcing Congress' laws, or of trying and convicting violators. For these reasons, as well as its inability to tax directly, the Congress was ineffective. The powers, although given on paper, were not "fully and effectually" given. Washington then alludes to the fear that prevented the states from establishing such an effective government. He locates the root of that fear in the Articles' decision to vest all national power in "a single body of men," the Congress. This suggests one of the most important features of the new Constitution, the separation of powers. "Hence results the necessity of a different organization."

After mentioning the great obstacles posed by the different particular interests of the states, Washington continues in the letter to inform the Congress of what the Convention believed was at stake:

> In all our deliberations on this subject we kept steadily in our view, that which appears to us the greatest interest of every true American, the consolidation of our Union, in which is involved our prosperity, felicity, safety, perhaps our national existence. This important consideration, seriously and deeply impressed on our minds, led each State in the Convention to be less rigid on points of inferior magnitude, than might have been otherwise expected....
> – George Washington, Letter of Transmittal

The immediate goal of the Constitution is the "consolidation" of the Union. By making the national government capable of carrying out its functions, the Constitution, it was hoped, would strengthen the Union among the states. By so doing, the prosperity, "felicity" (happiness) and safety of all Americans would be enhanced. If the Union were not strengthened, the Convention feared that the nation might cease to exist, as the states, with no effective limit to their power, began to act as "Free and Independent States" with regard to each other.

An important way in which the Constitution forms a "more perfect union" is contained in the Preamble itself. Unlike the Articles, which were established by the states, the Constitution is established by the People. Of course, the states only acted in virtue of the power granted them by their respective peoples, and so even the Articles were indirectly an act of the People of the United States. But the Constitution, in its Preamble, claims itself to be a direct act of the People of the United States. It was to be ratified by special conventions called in each state for the purpose of accepting the Constitution. That means that the authority given the federal compact came from the People in the several states, not their legislatures. We will return to this later.

Given their view of the powers government needed to be effective, it was crucial to the framers that the Constitution emanate directly from the People. The new government would have the power to tax directly. It would have the power to enforce its laws on recalcitrant individuals and even states. It would be able to judge and imprison offenders against its laws. Its laws would be the "supreme law of the land," having precedence over state laws. Such authority over individuals and states could only come directly from the People.

ESTABLISH JUSTICE

One great difficulty confronting a student of the Preamble is that its terms are very general. "Justice" is a prime example. It is a term that means many different things to many different people. Can one find a meaning that would be common enough to be accepted, but not so vague as to be useless?

Perhaps we can, especially if we think back on the Declaration's distinction between Peoples that are independent of each other and those that are bound together. Independent Peoples or States act together by means of alliances or treaties. In case of serious differences, they must either come to an agreement or go to war with each other. Smaller, weaker nations depend for their existence on the goodwill of the more powerful nations.

Within a nation, however, disputes between individuals or communities are settled in courts. Judges and juries make judgments according to established laws. Disturbers of the peace are arrested and punished by officers who act according to the laws. The small and the weak are now protected by the laws.

Justice, then, means the rule of law. The rule of law is a guarantee that judgments will be applied impartially, and hence the image of Justice is of a goddess who is blind-folded. Remember also that there is a law higher than the laws made by governments, the natural law. This means that the intention of the positive laws is understood to be consonant with that of the higher law.

Thinking along these lines, we can see that this second purpose statement describes the whole effort of the Constitution. A more perfect union demands a stronger, more effective government. But that government must use its strength to rule according to law, not to carry out the current passions of those who wield that power. The very act of establishing a Constitution, which is a set of laws specifying the scope and procedures of exercising power, is an act of establishing justice, or the rule of law. Perhaps that is why the same word, "establish," is used in the Preamble in reference to both "justice" and "this Constitution."

DOMESTIC TRANQUILLITY & DEFENSE

By creating the powers of an effective national government limited by law, the Constitution itself goes a long way toward strengthening the Union and establishing justice. Officials appointed according to the Constitution will be able to bring about the next two ends mentioned in the Preamble.

The greatest danger to life, liberty and property comes from men who will use force to seize them from each other. They might be other men living in society who refuse to live according to law, or they might be other Peoples formed in their own societies. A fundamental role of any government is to ensure that in neither case is force allowed to triumph. By organizing the power of the people as a whole, the government can take effective measures to keep the peace at home and defend itself against enemies abroad. In regard to these ends, it is worth reminding ourselves that the Preamble does not create any powers; it only defines the purpose of the powers granted to the national government in the body of the Constitution.

With regard to the common defense, the national government has preeminent jurisdiction. It can raise troops necessary for war, and it can assume command of the state militias when necessary. With regard to domestic peace, on the other hand, the national government is limited to the cases in which a national law is violated. Murder, robbery, disturbing the peace, and many other crimes do not ordinarily involve the federal government.

THE GENERAL WELFARE

"Welfare" is a term that today usually refers to federal and state government programs that provide financial support to those in need. That is definitely not the sense the word has here.

"Welfare" here means "well being." We have seen similar terms used throughout the texts we have been considering. "Happiness," "felicity," "prosperity." Clearly, our founders realized that men wish not only to live, but to live well. And they thought that men formed societies because they make both living and good living possible. So beyond the safety of its citizens ("domestic tranquility" and "common defense"), the government formed by the Constitution is to act to promote the happiness of its citizens.

Of course, this end is limited by the powers enumerated in the Constitution. The government, for instance, can't eliminate state governments in order to bring about happiness. Nor can it act in favor of one state over another. In order to indicate these limitations, "welfare" is qualified by the term "general." The federal government receives powers to act in those matters where the People's welfare can best be served by acting altogether for goods that benefit the whole nation.

THE BLESSINGS OF LIBERTY

If we look at Article I, Section 8, where powers are specified which are to promote the "general welfare," we see that many concern the material prosperity of the nation. A common government that could regulate commerce, establish a uniform currency, and grant patents to inventors would provide excellent opportunities for private citizens and corporations to develop the abundant natural resources of the nation for the ultimate benefit of all.

Does the national government have no concern about higher goods? The Preamble points beyond material concerns in its last purpose phrase—"secure the blessings of liberty to ourselves and our posterity." What are the blessings of liberty? If liberty means the power and right to act according to one's choices, then the blessings of liberty include all that proceed from the free choice and cooperation of private men—religion, education, the fine arts, practical charity. Unlike the Europeans, most Americans had come to the conclusion that these goods were better attained by free, private associations than by government patronage or regulation. Government was necessary in part to make secure the freedom of its citizens to pursue these goals.

The Union itself, whose maintenance is the chief end of the Constitution, enhanced liberty. The prospect for individuals to achieve happiness is far greater in an extended society. Citizens of Virginia could attend the fine universities in Massachusetts without passports (Robert E. Lee, for example, would send one of his sons to Harvard); citizens of Connecticut could move to South Carolina if the refined society of the landed gentry were more to their taste. National churches or other organizations could be formed, with greater power to achieve their goals than a relatively small society such as Rhode Island or even Virginia would permit. By facilitating harmony and friendship among the states, the federal government would secure and enhance the liberty of its citizens.

Finally, we should notice that the government should secure the "blessings" of liberty.

Freedom makes the greatest goods possible, but it can also be abused. The founders were under no illusion about the evils that can and sometimes do result from a free society. But freedom is not desired for the sake of these evils, nor even solely for its own sake, sweet though the savor of liberty is. Freedom is also, and perhaps chiefly, desirable because of the good things that it alone can produce. The government is to make secure liberty for the sake of the blessings. To the extent that a free man uses his freedom to the harm of others, the government is to resist him.

The federal government has undergone tremendous changes over the course of its existence. Eighteenth century Americans would undoubtedly be shocked at the function it plays in our society today. Some of its metamorphosis has come about through amendments, such as the Fourteenth, Sixteenth, and Seventeenth Amendments. More changes have come through adapting the existing Constitution to the perceived needs of different times. Some changes have undoubtedly bettered our nation; some may have made it worse. In order to judge properly those changes, and to make good decisions in the circumstances we face today, officials must understand its purposes. Lose sight of the end, and all is lost.

The first Congress under the Constitution faced tremendous financial difficulties arising from the war and from mismanagement under the Articles. Alexander Hamilton proposed rectifying the situation by the creation of a Bank of the United States. Congress passed legislation enacting the proposal. Hamilton claimed Congress was authorized to do this to promote the general welfare and specifically, under the powers enumerated and implied in Article I, Section 8. After an express enumeration of powers granted Congress, Article 8 goes on to add, "[Congress may] make all such laws which shall be necessary and proper for carrying into execution the foregoing powers...." The key words are "necessary and proper," since they imply non-enumerated powers. Both Jefferson and James Madison objected that Congress could justify any action whatever if it understood "necessary and proper" so broadly. President Washington asked for written advice from both sides, and chose to sign the Bank Bill into law. *Federalist* 44 addresses this issue of "implied powers." Was Hamilton right? Was Madison? Was either man thinking about the issue in terms of the spirit of the laws, or of ends?

In arguing for the fundamental role of the American People in authorizing the Constitution, we noted that, though the states did not ratify through their legislatures, neither was there a national plebiscite or national convention for that purpose, but state conventions. And the Constitution only came into effect in a state once that state, together with eight others, had already ratified by convention. This ratification process seems to acknowledge some continuation of a kind of sovereignty which the Peoples of the several states had under the Articles. And, while federal law is supreme, (Article VI, section 2) there appears to be a division of sovereignty between the states and the national government in the American Constitutional order. Does this make the Union under the Constitution a pact between independent nations, or one nation, or some third thing?

The author inclines strongly to the view that the union is one nation, meant to be perpetual, with divided sovereignty, apportioned according to diverse objects, and with federal supremacy. Still, how this works out precisely is a matter for deep reflection and even controversy, and we do not mean to settle the question in this book.[8]

THE STRUCTURE ACTUALLY ESTABLISHED IN THE CONSTITUTION

Before we explore the mechanics of the government, let's recall what was said about proper government in the Declaration:

1. Receiving their authority from the consent of the governed, governments have for their ends the safety and happiness of the people. Their safety consists in the defense of their natural rights to life, liberty and the pursuit of happiness. Their happiness extends beyond property, to include fulfillment of duty, honor and justice.
2. Governments are judged by their fidelity to the law of nature and of nature's God respecting all men, and accordingly, by their effectiveness in attaining the happiness and safety of the people.

8 The inquiring reader is urged to read and meditate on Federalist 39, 40 and 43, especially the end of 43, and to read Daniel Webster's *Second Reply to Hayne,* written in 1830, as well as Lincoln's First inaugural and his July 4th 1861 message to Congress. For the position contrary to Webster's, consult *Declaration of the Immediate Causes Which Induce and Justify the Secession of South Carolina from the Federal Union,* or any of the other 3 such declarations by seceding states. A thorough analysis of the question, concluding that the Union is not a compact of sovereign states, may be found in *A New Birth of Freedom* by Harry Jaffa.

3. In the Declaration, the colonists compacted themselves as one People, recognizing that their safety and happiness depended on their national unity.
4. The importance of prudence in all political decisions is emphasized, as is,
5. The separation of legislative, executive and judicial powers.

Now let's turn to the government established by the Constitution.

There is a fundamental principle behind the first Declaration principle just listed that helps to explain, at least in part, many of its features: Because governments exist for the good of a free People, the People, to the extent that they can, must be in charge. In the Preamble, we saw that the People intend to secure their safety, their liberty and their happiness through the Constitution. The experience of the British and American peoples had led them to realize the importance of having those whose interests or goods are involved be the source of this deliberation and choice. After all, who is more likely to take care of what is yours than you? So the Constitution involves the people directly in governing.

Article One establishes that one part of the legislative body, the House of Representatives, will be directly elected by the people. Article Two establishes that the President shall be chosen by electors appointed "in such manner as the legislature of [each state] may direct." If the People of a particular state want to directly vote for President, and if they elect a state legislature that conforms to this desire, they can choose their electors directly.

The House and the President have the most direct effect on the People, the House being the source of all taxation, the President having the executive power of the sword. In the original wording of the Constitution, other important governmental bodies are indirectly appointed by the People. Senators are chosen by their state legislature, which is itself elected by the People; while the President, with the Senate, appoints Justices. Both hold their office, ultimately, from the People, but both stand at some distance from them, their longer terms (six years for Senators, life tenure for the Justices) ensuring some insulation from popular will. How is this consistent with the principle that the People should rule?

We have seen earlier that the Americans were well aware of the disastrous consequences of popular rule in ancient times. Most men are prone to quick judgments, especially when they are affected by their passions—fear, greed, jealousy, vengeance, or even pity, sympathy or love. Quick judgments often lead to great errors. (Remember King Herod and John the Baptist, or King Midas and his touch.) This is especially true when they don't have all the facts. Think of hearing of a terrible crime on television or the radio. Many people immediately want the person accused to be put away. But they don't know all the facts. It sometimes turns out that the person wasn't guilty, or there were mitigating circumstances. Consider John Adams' brave legal defense of the redcoats in the Boston Massacre! That is why such matters are settled in courts, and not by having buttons on our remote controls that will allow us to say whether the person should be convicted and punished or not.

While early Americans firmly believed that they could rule themselves, they knew that important decisions take time, time to let passions cool, to discover the facts, to discuss the matter with friends or trusted counselors. In other words, important decisions must be the result of prudent deliberation, the fourth Declaration principle noted above.

Most of us don't have the time or inclination to deliberate properly about all the affairs of government. So we appoint certain people to act on our behalf, in much the same way as we might appoint a lawyer to argue for us in court. A small number of experienced men, devoted to the work of governing, makes for effective deliberation.

The need for deliberation also explains in part the fifth Declaration principle, and why the Constitution separated the legislature into a House and Senate, and separates the law-making branch from both the executive and the judicial branches. All three functions are needed for government to be successful. Laws must be passed, then carried out, with offenders judged and punished. Further, each branch can affect the other in its own sphere; the President can veto legislation, the Congress can refuse to confirm Judges, the courts can declare legislation unconstitutional. This means that, under the Constitution, change will take time. The more serious the change, the longer it will take.

In order for serious changes in governmental practice to take place, all three branches have to work together. If all three powers are united in a monarch, all one has to do is convince the king that something should be done, and it is done.

Under the Constitution, even if a majority of the people elect enough Representatives to get the House to pass a law, it can't change the Senate all at once.

If the law is radical and uncertain, it will have to be moderated to get the Senate to agree, or else the People will have to show by their election of state legislators (who used to appoint the Senators) in the next few elections that they continue to want the change. The People will also have to elect a President who will not veto the measure, or else get two-thirds of both Houses to override the veto. All of these measures gain time, which is crucial to successful deliberation. If the change is not for the good of the People, then they generally won't continue to want it for the time required to make it.

We can easily imagine what the Constitution's framers would think of Senators, Presidents, or even Representatives who made their decisions according to the latest opinion poll.

The Constitutional structure also tries to ensure that changes are for the good of the whole People the third named Declaration principle, and not just of one segment which might have a majority. The Senators were originally appointed directly by the state legislatures, and each state still has an equal number of votes in the United States Senate. The Electoral College system forces the President to win a majority of electors from the states rather than a majority of the popular vote. These measures and others ensured that a more single-minded section of the country, say the Northeast or the South or the Coastal states, has to convince a portion of the rest of the country that what it wants is good for everyone. These regional checks built into the Constitution have played an important role in keeping our country united.

So far we have seen how the Constitution allows the People to use government structures in a deliberate manner to bring about the general welfare. How does it protect liberty? Most importantly, it places rule in the hands of the People as a whole. No greater protection for freedom can be found than by placing power in the hands of those who would be most affected by its loss. The separation of powers strengthens popular authority by placing hindrances in the paths of ambitious men who might want to take it away. Notice, for instance, that the President begins his term by swearing to "preserve, protect and defend the Constitution of the United

States." The President is authorized by this to resist any attempts on the parts of the other branches or by the states to violate the Constitution and seize power from the People. Although ordinarily we think of the Supreme Court as the body that determines what the Constitution means, the President and Congress have a solemn duty to resist the Court when it tries to usurp powers not given to it in the Constitution. Andrew Jackson and Abraham Lincoln both resisted Courts that they thought had exceeded their proper roles.

Specific guarantees of liberty are also built into the Constitution. Although they don't stand out like the Bill of Rights, they have been very important in maintaining peace and freedom in our country. For instance, the definition of treason (Article III, section 3), is strictly limited. Only actual aid to a national enemy can be considered treason. Ambitious rulers have often used accusations of treason as a way to get rid of political enemies and terrify the populace. Any statements, even private conversations, in which the sovereign's decisions were criticized, were used as grounds for punishment. The Constitution forbids such tyrannical acts.

Other safeguards include taxation in proportion to population, ensuring that no one area or group of people be singled out for unfair treatment. Trial by jury is guaranteed. Religious tests for office are forbidden; and no titles of nobility can be granted.

There is also a guarantee of "a republican form of government" to the states, (Art. IV, sect. 4). What might be meant by "republican" in this section? Does this not limit the sovereignty of the people in a state? Is it not a *prohibition* against their choosing another form of state government? Could a mere league or treaty between sovereign nations include such a guarantee or prohibition?

Finally, as Publius was to argue in *Federalist* 10 and 51, the very extent and diversity of occupation and interest in an extended republic helps to ensure liberty by placing checks on narrow or regional commercial and political factions. Compromise, collaboration, and appeals to reason will be needed to make the wheels of legislation and administration turn; it will be hard, in a vast and diverse political community, for designing men and self-interested factions to have their way when others are watching, jealous for their own liberty and interest.

THE BILL OF RIGHTS

As Americans, we are justly proud of our Constitution, which has been a bulwark of our freedom for two centuries. Through the structures it established, it has guaranteed popular government by bringing to it a stability unknown to previous history. However, when Americans think of safeguards to liberty, we often think of something not originally in the Constitution, namely the Bill of Rights, the first ten amendments to the Constitution. With their guarantees of freedom of religion and of the press, of bearing arms, of due process, and so on, it is no wonder that we would consider them a bulwark against governmental and majority tyranny.

As we have seen, the Constitution contains some determinate restrictions on the federal government, but the Constitutional Convention deliberately refrained from including a Bill of Rights in the original document. The most severe criticism of the Constitution came from this omission. Indeed, the lack of a bill of rights endangered ratification in a number of states. The intensity of this criticism led to promises that a bill of rights would be included after ratification, by way of amendment.

And this promise was kept. The first ten amendments are a powerful sign that the Constitution is really an act of the People, not only of the Convention.

Why did the Convention, so wise in many ways, not include a bill of rights in the Constitution? The best defense of their decision was given by Publius in *Federalist* 84.

> "I go farther and affirm that … bills of rights are not only unnecessary in the proposed Constitution, but would even be dangerous."

Publius argued that they are *unnecessary* because, under the Constitution, the rule of the People was guaranteed. No better safeguard to liberty can be found than the People themselves. Even advocates of a bill of rights agreed that no substitute could be found for the exertion of the popular will in defense of the People's liberties. A bill would simply make it easy for the People to tell when its liberties were in danger. As Richard Henry Lee put it, "…They become visible boundaries, constantly seen by all, and any transgression of them is immediately discovered: They serve as sentinels for the people at all times, and especially in those unavoidable intervals of inattention."

But why would a bill of rights be *dangerous* to liberty? Publius explained the danger this way. Those clamoring for a bill of rights had a false notion of the Constitution. Through the Constitution, the People grants certain, definite powers to the federal government. If the People does not grant the power, the government does not have it. The government is like a lawyer, whose actions on behalf of his client are limited to what is explicitly authorized by the client. A lawyer doesn't need to be told that he can't sign your checks; he knows he cannot unless you grant him that power specifically.

But if your lawyer has a letter from you telling him not to sign a particular check, then he might argue, from that letter, that he did have the authority to sign other checks. Limits on a power imply that the power exists, indeed has been granted. In Publius' words,

> They would contain various exceptions to powers which are not granted; and, on this very account, would afford a colorable pretext to claim more than were granted. For why declare that things shall not be done which there is no power to do?

The first Congress tried to overcome the danger pointed out by Publius through what became the Ninth and Tenth Amendments. The Tenth Amendment makes explicit the limited nature of the authority of the federal government. It has only those powers that the People delegate to it, and it can only perform those functions it has been authorized and empowered by the People to perform. All other powers are left in the hands of the People or the states. This amendment aims at maintaining the residual sovereignty of the states, and the natural rights of individual citizens. It intends to prevent the federal government from thinking it may do anything it thinks desirable. We did not expect or want the federal government to remedy all evil whatsoever, even if the price had to be forbidding it from a wider latitude for doing good. For instance, in the early 20th Century, a substantial majority had come to think that drinking alcoholic beverages was an evil which should be prohibited by law. But Congress, not having been given this authority specifically, could not legislate such a ban. To do so, the Constitution had to be amended, as it was, in 1919. The experiment in total prohibition was judged unsatisfactory, and the amendment repealed in 1933. Since then, states and local communities have decided the issue for themselves.

The Ninth Amendment was added for similar reasons. But whereas the Tenth limits government powers, the Ninth asserts the priority of natural rights, inhering in the People. "The enumeration in the Constitution, of certain rights, shall not be construed to deny or disparage others retained by the people." The Constitution is not the source of our fundamental rights. As we have seen from the Declaration, the source of our rights is found in a much higher authority than the Constitution. They come from our nature as men, created in the image of God. The rights to life, liberty and the pursuit of happiness are not explicit in the Constitution, but they still exist, as the Constitution itself presupposes them.

In spite of the precautions in the Ninth and Tenth Amendments, some of Publius' fears have come to pass. Today, many of us look to government, especially the federal government, to solve all our problems. What, we ask, is the President, or the Congress, going to do about the economy? What are they going to do about education, violent crime, drugs, offensive television programs, smoking, unhealthy foods, etc.? If there is a good to be done, or a wrong to be righted, we expect the federal government to do it, whether the power to do such things is found in the Constitution or not. Maybe we think too highly of the Constitution, imagining that if a good can be done, the Constitution must have given the federal government the power to do it.

The Bill of Rights has played a two-fold role in this evolution. One we have just noted. It was meant to check these developments, but did so only imperfectly. In spite of the Ninth and Tenth Amendments, the political branches of the federal government, the Congress and the Executive, have tended to assume powers and duties not granted in the Constitution.

The other role played by the Bill has been, and remains to this day, deeply controversial. The Supreme Court has used the first ten amendments, and other amendments passed after the Bill of Rights, to block countless acts of Congress, state legislatures, popular initiatives, and city governments. Since the Supreme Court is a federal organ, this has meant the extension of federal authority over state and local authority. Since the judiciary is the least accountable branch, it has constituted, even at the federal level, a veto over the popular will, as expressed by elected representatives.

Accordingly, it has been the means of forcing changes on an unwilling society. Some of these changes have been for the better. When state governments and other local sources of authority refuse to right notable injustices, such as slavery or segregation, then the People will find a champion somewhere. Slavery was ended by war and amendment, but segregation was struck down by the courts. Some changes at the state and local level, in the mode of election of state and municipal governments, in the role of religion in public schools, in the authority of local school boards and local police forces, and many other matters, have been instances of the federal courts' applying the words of the Bill of Rights to matters the Framers may well have meant to be left to the states and the People.

Given the tremendous impact the Bill of Rights has had in our day, perhaps the Declaration of Independence is most immediately important in helping us to understand those amendments properly. Let us look at a few of them, and see how Declaration principles preclude the most extreme of today's interpretations. We begin with religion and civil society, and hence with the First Amendment.

It is worth noting that the First Amendment yokes two things, which could have required separate amendments. The First Amendment prohibits Congress from establishing any religion or from restraining the free exercise of religion. *And* it forbids Congress from abridging the rights of free speech, a free press, and free public assembly. These latter are all political rights, and proper to a regime in which sovereignty rests in the People. To vote well, to give reasoned consent, a citizen must be able to assemble with others, he must have access to a free press, and such a citizen must be able to speak freely in public. By coupling promotion of a soul's freedom to worship God as it sees fit and promotion of a citizen's free political judgment, the amendment seems to hint that the two operate in tandem in securing the blessings of liberty. In this light it is worth wondering if in the Framers' view you could have political liberty without religion and religious liberty.

The amendment restricted Congress only. The states could, and many did, have religious establishments. The decision to end all establishments came, state by state, by legislation, not judicial action, over the next 40 years or so. And the restriction on establishment at the federal level was not understood to prohibit national days of fasting and prayer, chaplains in Congress and the armed forces, and many other policies meant to encourage and foster religion. That was natural enough, since the American Republic, in its Declaration, saw its foundation in an endowment from God, and since nearly all the founders thought that religion was a prop and stay of general morality and virtue. And these they thought necessary in order to sustain political liberty. Such was the original understanding of the relation of the amendment to "separation of church and state."

In the last fifty years, however, chiefly through the agency of the courts, the First Amendment has been used to ease religion out of the role it had peaceably enjoyed in public life for more than a century. Christmas displays are banished from public property; prayers in public schools, or before the football games their teams play, are forbidden; laws regulating risky and peculiar sexual behavior or other activity are overturned, apparently on the grounds that the preferred, safe and sane conduct is not in conformity with nature, but only particular religious strictures; charities and voluntary associations, like the Boy Scouts, find difficulty in cooperating with government agencies because they stand for a faith-based moral code. The thinking on which these policies and judgments are based seems to be that the First Amendment, understood as requiring an absolute "separation of church and state," forbids deference to the Creator in American public life.

Little of this would have happened had we read the Constitution in the light of the Declaration. If, as the Declaration plainly states, our fundamental rights come from God, then there is no way that He can be excluded from public life, or that religion, which teaches the respect for God and consequently our rights, can be treated as a public enemy. To do so is to undermine the very basis of our society and guarantee of our liberties.

Thinking from the Declaration, we can better understand what the Amendment really means to prevent. In their former countries Americans knew the horrors of wars fought by those so sure they knew which church is the true one that they were ready, nay eager, to destroy those they could not persuade. The First Amendment prevents Congress from supporting one church against another, and from punishing anyone for not believing or worshiping as a majority might think they should. The Episcopalians cannot be favored over the Catholics, Presbyterians over Jews. The Amendment does not, however, prevent Congress from honoring or otherwise encouraging religion generally.

"In God We Trust" proclaim our dollars; our armed services are supplied with chaplains at public expense; sessions of the Supreme Court begin with the words, "God save this honorable court!" There are disputable matters in this field, and men of goodwill may reasonably differ about them. But the first amendment certainly was not intended to prevent a statue of Moses holding the Ten Commandments from being displayed in a courthouse, or a public school teacher from handing out to his students extracts from American statesmen in which the religious roots of republican liberty are stressed. A republic founded on self-evident truths that include the divine source of rights cannot enshrine a right to exclude God altogether from the public square.

The Second Amendment protects the right of the people to keep and bear arms. Why did Americans see this as crucial? Nowadays some people might argue that individuals don't need to have weapons, because we have strong armies that defend us from foes abroad and police that apprehend the criminals among us. Maybe so. The Second Amendment sees the question otherwise. As the Declaration states so clearly, a government itself can become tyrannical, and the People have a right to abolish their government when it becomes tyrannical. Moreover, it is a longstanding view of the natural law, and one found in Locke, among others, that when the police power is absent, the individual has a right of self-defense. But how can men exercise those rights if they have no arms? The American Revolution would never have succeeded if the multitude of citizens had not been well armed and able to use those arms.

The Second Amendment speaks of "bearing arms," which means carrying them in public, and it speaks of militias. The American Revolution never would have succeeded if the citizens had not been regulated in militias. The "minutemen" were ordinary, but armed, citizens, ready at a moment's notice from their elected leaders to resist in a body the armies of the king. They were a tolerably "well regulated militia." The Second Amendment exists to sustain the practical possibility of precisely such a just rebellion, and to instill fear in potential tyrants. We must admit that allowing ordinary citizens to have weapons might be dangerous. But the Framers thought that allowing the government to command a standing army while at the same time disarming its citizens would surely invite tyranny.

Amendments four through eight protect citizens against abuses of legal and police powers. Government officials cannot invade or spy on the lives of ordinary citizens without having some definite, particular reason to suspect them of a crime. Citizens are entitled to a speedy, fair trial by a jury. Punishments and fines are not to be cruel, unusual, or arbitrary. The Seventh Amendment, which restricts judicial review of matters of fact in civil cases provides an interesting instance of the truth of Publius' observation in *Federalist* 84. The omission of a similar restriction concerning matters of law led to a transfer of the function of interpretation of those matters from juries to judges. The result was to make the law more consistent, but also less 'populist," as juries lost an important power

In undoubtedly the most controversial interpretation of the Bill of Rights in our century, the Supreme Court determined in *Roe v. Wade* that these amendments, together with an open-ended reading of the unenumerated rights of the Ninth Amendment, guarantee a mother's "right" to kill her unborn child. The Declaration's assertion of the fundamental right to life militates against such a reading of the meaning of the Constitution. The Preamble itself points to legal duties towards, and rights of, the unborn when it speaks of securing the "Blessings of Liberty to ourselves and our posterity." Surely the first of "our posterity" is the innocent child in the womb. Moreover, the Declaration asserts that our fundamental rights, including the right to life, come from God. Can these fundamental rights be taken away without violation of the higher law that makes all our human laws possible?

We can see by now that the Constitution as a whole was the product of prudent men. They saw clearly the goals they wanted to achieve, and they drew from their experience and the experience of the ages to establish a practical and effective instrument of popular rule and national unity. The Constitution is a great instrument of a free People.

But in order for us to use the Constitution properly, we have to keep before us the goals that it is meant to achieve. These are most clearly stated in the Declaration of Independence: to maintain the rights to life, liberty and the pursuit of happiness; to promote the safety and happiness of the People. The Constitution presupposes these goals. It does not, for the most part, determine what things are just and right and good; it merely provides the means to bring them about, especially by making it possible for the People to exercise effective authority.

Over the years, justices, presidents, senators, and representatives have all had to try to use this great instrument in different ways. They have used its powers from day to day, struggled to interpret it in very different situations from that of the founders, and have adapted it by numerous amendments when it seemed to be inadequate. Through it all, the American people have had to judge these efforts, giving their blessing or reacting in outrage. Often, people would read the Constitution apart from the Declaration, as though it were the sole foundation of our country. In the most important decisions, this inevitably fails. When we forget to read the Constitution as the instrument of a People of the Declaration, we make many grave mistakes.

We will consider some of these in the next chapter.

CHAPTER 7
THE STAIN OF SLAVERY

> ... He has waged cruel war against human nature itself, violating its most sacred rights of life and liberty in the persons of a distant people who never offended him, captivating & carrying them into slavery in another hemisphere, or to incur miserable death in their transportation thither.
> – Jefferson, *first draft of the Declaration of Independence*, 1776

> ... And can the liberties of a nation be thought secure when we have removed their only firm basis, a conviction in the minds of the people that these liberties are the gift of God? That they are not to be violated but with his wrath? Indeed, I tremble for my country when I reflect that God is just: that his justice cannot sleep for ever: that considering numbers, nature, and natural means only, a revolution of the wheel of fortune, an exchange of situation, is among possible events: that it may become probable by supernatural interference! The Almighty has no attribute which can take side with us in such a contest.
>
> ... I think a change is already perceptible, since the origin of the present revolution. The spirit of the master is abating, that of the slave rising from the dust, his condition mollifying, the way I hope preparing, under the auspices of heaven, for a total emancipation, and that this is disposed, in the order of events, to be with the consent of the masters, rather than by their extirpation.
> – Jefferson, *Notes on the State of Virginia*, Query XVIII, written in 1782

The American Republic, born in 1776 and confirmed in the Constitution of 1787, sparked the wonder and interest of the world. It was to be the test of self-government based on equal natural rights. The Founders had declared that, "all men are created equal." Yet many of them, Jefferson included, held their fellow men in bondage, in slavery. Their Constitution counted each slave at the rate of three-fifths of a free person in apportioning taxes and representatives to the lower house of Congress. It required that "... [a] person held to service or labor [i.e., a slave], in one state, escaping into another ... shall be delivered up on claim of the party to whom such service or labor may be due." It promised not to interfere with "the migration or importation of such persons as the States now existing shall think proper to admit [i.e., slaves] prior to the year 1808."

These things have led many to speak harshly of the great charter of our Republic. Frederick Douglass, the formidable black orator, writer, and statesman, said this about the Constitution: "Liberty and Slavery—opposite as Heaven and Hell—are both in the Constitution." And similar criticisms persist in our times. The following passage is taken from a widely used contemporary textbook[9]: "Whereas earlier the Declaration of Independence had so eloquently proclaimed that 'all men are created equal,' the delegates to the Constitutional Convention put political expediency before the immorality of slavery."

Why did the Founders act as they did? Were they so blinded by racial prejudice as not to believe the black men and women they held in slavery to be human beings? This second question admits of an easy answer. They knew that blacks were men. Jefferson's original draft of the Declaration, quoted above, goes on to denounce the king as, "Determined to keep open a market where MEN should be bought and sold...." The parts of the Constitution that recognize the institution of slavery and grant certain protections to the slave owner consistently refer to the slave as a "person," and what beast or mere article of property, what indeed but a human being or something higher than a human being has ever been called a person? The language of the Constitution does not even bear the words slave or slavery, as though, as Lincoln was to remark later, the Framers did not wish to stain the purity of the Federal Constitution with the ugly name of an unjust institution. Alexander Hamilton, writing to John Jay in 1779, urged the emancipation of those black slaves who had served in the continental Army

9 *American Government: Roots and Reform*, O'Connor and Sabato.

(and there were many of them) in these words, "... the dictates of humanity and true policy equally interest me in favor of this unfortunate class of men." It is needless to insist on this point further. Evidence abounds that the men of the founding generation, whatever they may have thought about social equality or differences in natural talents, universally recognized that their black slaves were men.

How, then, could they justify their actions, especially the Constitutional provisions that protected the slave owners? How persuasive was that justification? And what does it mean for us in understanding America, its history and its principles?

We should first look at how the generation that fought for independence, the generation of the Declaration, dealt with slavery in America. It is a stirring but incomplete tale of progress and partial victory, but also of exhaustion and defeat. It shows the power of ideas, but also the need for perseverance and wise statesmanship. Lack of that perseverance ushered in the crisis of the "house divided," and the bloodshed of the Civil War. But without the success that was attained, Jefferson's brooding remarks about Divine retribution for injustice would have foretold an even more tragic outcome.

As with the revolutionary movement itself, so with the question of slavery we would do well to look first to the churches and sermons of the day to discover the motives and ideas that were leading Americans to dream of and fight for liberty for the slaves. Congregationalist Levi Hart, writing in 1774, put the case in the fervid rhetoric of the day:

> What have the unhappy Africans, committed against the inhabitants of the British colonies and islands in the West Indies to authorize us to seize them and transport them a thousand leagues into a strange land, and enslave them for life?... What inconsistence and self-contradiction is this!... When, O when shall the happy day come, that Americans shall be consistently engaged in the cause of liberty?

Baptist preacher John Allen called the keeping of African slaves an "iniquitous and disgraceful practice." Allen, Hart, and like-minded preachers pointedly declared that the charges of tyranny and slavery that their fellow colonists had levied against the king were, as Samuel Hopkins put it,

> ... lighter than a feather compared to their [the slaves'] heavy doom, and may be called liberty and happiness when contrasted with the most abject slavery and unutterable wretchedness to which they are subjected....

It is a teaching of both Classical and Judeo-Christian morality that doing unjust things harms not only the victim, but also the doer. Statesmen as well as preachers held to this teaching. Madison said this, at the Convention:

> The poor despise labor when performed by slaves.... They [slaves] produce the most pernicious effect on manners. Every master of slaves is born a petty tyrant. They bring the judgement of heaven on a Country. As nations can not be rewarded or punished in the next world, they must be in this. By an inevitable chain of causes and effects providence punishes national sins by national calamities....

Such ideas, widely promulgated in pamphlets and sermons, were not without effect. Before the revolution, Massachusetts' legislature had twice voted to abolish the slave trade, only to be thwarted by the Royal Governor's veto. Momentum for freedom grew during and after the revolution. In April 1776, Congress voted that "no slaves be imported into any of the thirteen colonies." Local action in New Hampshire and Massachusetts effectively ended slavery in those states in the 1780's. Pennsylvania passed a gradual emancipation law in 1780. Jefferson himself introduced a proposal for abolition in the Virginia legislature in 1778, and in 1784, he drafted legislation for the Congress that would have banned slavery in all the territories of the United States, including the "southwest", i.e. the areas that would become the states of Alabama, Mississippi, Tennessee, and Kentucky. The measure failed by just one vote. Even the slave states of the deep South had all abolished the slave trade, though not slavery itself, by 1798.

The Northwest Ordinance of 1787 is a striking witness to the moral authority of Declaration principles in the national government, as well as the federal government's constitutional authority to ban slavery in national territories. In that year, under the Articles of Confederation, Congress forbade slavery in the land that would subsequently become the states of Ohio, Indiana, Illinois, Michigan, and Wisconsin. Unlike the Southwest territory, which was ceded to the national government by slave-holding states on the condition that slavery be permitted, the Northwest was essentially under the tutelage of the national government. Congress, free to act, enacted freedom.

Two centuries and more after these events, we tend to view the slavery question through the lens of the Civil War, as a sectional issue only that pitted North against South. True though it was that slavery was concentrated in the Southern states, it is important to remember that all thirteen of the original states were slave states at the outbreak of the revolution.

Abolition anywhere, North or South, entailed struggle and sacrifice, often of the greater part of one's own or a neighbor's wealth. So did voluntary release from slavery, a practice known as "manumission." Even so, by 1810, slavery was abolished or on the road to abolition in the majority of the thirteen original states, and over 100,000 former slaves were free men in the South, more than the nearly 80,000 in the North. Taken together, free blacks, North and South, amounted to about one eighth of the black population counted in that census.

None of this progress towards freedom would have happened without the force of the moral and religious convictions of the Americans of the revolutionary period or in the absence of their adherence to the principles of the Declaration. Twentieth century historian Bernard Bailyn, in his book on the origins of the American Revolution, puts it this way:

> [Slavery] had been subjected to severe pressure as a result of the extension of Revolutionary ideas, and it bore the marks ever after. As long as the institution lasted, the burden of proof would lie with its advocates to show why the statement 'all men are created equal' did not mean precisely what it said: all men, 'white or black.'

The logic of Bailyn's conclusion is sound only if we grant the Declaration's self-evident truth that it cites. As a political fact, it is sound only if statesmen take that truth as their pole star, and teach and proclaim it to citizens who also find it written in their hearts. Something was amiss in one or both of these conditions as the founding generation grew old and died.

The southward moving trend of abolition stopped, north of the Potomac River. No more states voluntarily ended the practice of human bondage after New Jersey's legislation of 1804. A weary Jefferson, no longer the sanguine young man who wrote the *Notes on the State of Virginia*, wrote this in his 83rd year:

> The revolution in public opinion which this cause [ending slavery] requires, is not to be expected in a day, or perhaps in an age; but time, which outlives all things, will outlive this evil also. My sentiments have been forty years before the public. Had I repeated them forty times, they would only have become the more stale and threadbare. Although I shall not live to see them consummated, they will not die with me; but living or dying, they will ever be in my most fervent prayer. This is written for yourself and not for the public....
>
> – Jefferson, *Letter to James Heaton*, Monticello, May 20, 1826

Six weeks and three days later, on July 4th, 1826, Thomas Jefferson died.

PRUDENCE, PRINCIPLE, AND HOPE

Let us review what we have concluded and what we want to ask. The founders knew perfectly well that black slaves were men. They knew that the institution of slavery contradicted the spirit of the Declaration. The generation of the Revolution abolished slavery in the North, and in the territory that the nation controlled. It outlawed the slave trade as soon as the Constitution allowed, in 1808. But it also gave Constitutional guarantees to the right of property in slaves, including the onerous duty of hunting down and returning escaped slaves. And in the South, where the bulk of the slaves lived, it failed to outlaw the practice.

What then were the Founders thinking?

THE POLICY OF THE FOUNDERS

A direct answer would be simple: to save the Union. A longer form of that answer would be, to preserve the principles of the Declaration, and act with prudence in the hope that the evil, if contained, would diminish and die.

In the previous section we have argued that slavery was in principle a problem for the whole American Nation. Among the reasons we gave were that all the states were originally slave states, and that the national legislative body, Congress, with Jefferson himself voting "aye," had passed the ban on slavery in the Northwest Ordinance. And of paramount importance, the basis for rejection of human slavery is the equality of men as a gift of God, a founding truth of the Republic. As a matter of practical politics, however, there was a strongly sectional color to the issue, one that it would have been unwise and even irresponsible for Madison and the other members of the Constitutional Convention to ignore. There was some trouble in ending slavery in Massachusetts, where the slave owners were few and the Declaration principles strong. It was much harder to do in New York; the Tories had been strong there, and the wealth represented by the more numerous slaves was considerable. Virginia, led by the redoubtable Jefferson, at least considered the question. But in the lower South, especially South Carolina and to a lesser degree Georgia, the task was practically impossible. More than half the human population of South Carolina consisted of black slaves, and Georgia, which had prohibited slavery up to 1751, was a rich agricultural frontier by 1787, filling up with plantation wealth and the attendant slaves, numbering about two-fifths of the total inhabitants as early as 1780. Such facts led Madison to say, of the debates at the Convention,

> … the real difference of interests lay, not between the large and small, but between the Northern and Southern states. The institution of slavery and its consequences formed the line of discrimination.

Individuals could manumit their slaves, and many, including George Washington, in his will, did so. But emancipation, even gradual emancipation, would not occur by the voluntary act of the states. In 1776 the charge against the king of "[waging] cruel war against human nature itself" in perpetuating the slave trade, had to be dropped from the Declaration, according to Jefferson, "in complaisance to S. Carolina and Georgia, who had never attempted to restrain the importation of slaves, and who on the contrary still wished to continue it."[10]

By the time of the Constitutional Convention, not only would South Carolina refuse to emancipate its own slaves, it would not, according to its delegates, John Rutledge and Charles Pinckney, stay in the Union if the slave trade was permanently abolished, or if there were no fugitive slave law. Pinckney declared in the Convention that, "South Carolina can never receive the plan if it prohibits the slave trade," while Rutledge, openly avowed that "humanity and religion have nothing to do with this question—interest alone is the governing principle with Nations—the true question at present is whether the Southern States shall or shall not be parties to the Union." The more moderate Hugh Williamson of North Carolina, himself on record as opposed to slavery in principle, declared that "the S. States could not be members of the Union if the clause [forbidding Congress from banning the slave trade] should be rejected."

Could America have enjoyed peace and prosperity in several distinct confederacies better than in one Union? Suppose that South Carolina and Georgia had formed a distinct republic in 1790. Would it not have been in their interest to reach a military and diplomatic understanding with Great Britain? What might the War of 1812 have looked like with British naval forces based in Charlestown harbor? Would a disunited America have had a greater chance of being drawn into the Napoleonic Wars, which convulsed Europe for the first decade and a half of the 19th century?

At the end of the second *Federalist*, Publius wrote,

> whenever the dissolution of the Union arrives, America will have reason to exclaim, in the words of the poet: 'FAREWELL! A LONG FAREWELL TO ALL MY GREATNESS.'

To establish the importance of the *Union* was the chief object of the first 22 of the papers, especially of the first ten.

10 Jefferson went on to mention that some Northerners were also hesitant about this condemnation because of their involvement in the slave trade. However, they were willing to act against their own economic interest by abolishing the slave trade once they had the chance.

We should remember what Publius said in the first issues of *The Federalist*, that the world was watching their experiment in republican government to decide the question of whether men could govern themselves by "reflection and choice," and that the "prosperity of America depended on its Union." The Convention was called to meet an emergency. The Articles were inept, and thus, the Union, and with it, the great experiment, was in danger. If there was no Union, Madison and the convention judged, there would be no durable and safe republican regime in the new world, and mankind would be the loser. Compromise was necessary, or there would be no "*novus ordo seclorum.*"

COMPROMISE AND HOPE

Pinckney, who was a patriot and had been a general in the Revolutionary War, wanted a strong Union, too. He may not have made good on his threats. In the event, he and his Southern brethren accepted a compromise and ratified the Constitution. The Southerners postponed the national ban on the slave trade until 1808 and obtained the fugitive slave clause. They did not get the term "legally" used to describe "persons held to service or labor." Those in the Convention who held to the natural law doctrine insisted that what was inherently unjust must never be termed "legal."

The slave states also won a major point on the issue of representation of their slave population in Congress and in electoral votes for the presidency. It seemed natural to many, most of all the enemies of slavery, that slaves should not be counted in calculating the states' shares in a Congress representing free citizens. Counting "all other persons" (note again how the Constitution recoils from even the words, 'slave' or 'slavery') as three-fifths of free persons was a concession to the South, which wanted the slaves to "stand on an equality with the whites," as Pinckney put it, in setting the states' representation and taxation. Gouverneur Morris, of Pennsylvania, whose sentiments on slavery may be judged from his calling it in the Convention debates, "a nefarious institution," opposed counting slaves at all, on the grounds that it would give "encouragement to the slave trade." Free blacks were, of course, counted as free persons.

Pinckney wanted, but did not obtain, an explicit statement that Congress could not abolish slavery. The Constitution was silent on this point until the Thirteenth Amendment directly outlawed the "nefarious institution" in 1865, after the Civil War. Benjamin Franklin seems to have thought the power to abolish slavery *did* exist in the Constitution. At least, that is a reasonable inference from his last great public act, in 1790. On February 12th of that year, a petition arrived in the House of Representatives, under the signature of Franklin, asking Congress to "take such measures in their wisdom, as the powers with which they are invested will authorize, for promoting the abolition of slavery...." The petition argued that Congress had power over slavery from the 'general welfare' clause of the Constitution. The petition was received by the House, over protests from Georgia and South Carolina, which did not even want it read or noticed, and a vigorous debate ensued.

Fearing the dissolution of the union in its infancy, the House, under the influence of James Madison, endorsed a report denying any federal power over slavery. The vote was 29–25. This effectively ended any abolition efforts by the national government until the Civil War, though some anti-slavery Congressmen argued, in the debates over the admission of Missouri in 1819–20, that the commerce clause gave Congress such power over a state. But the anti-slavery congressmen of 1820 never had the votes to put the interpretation to the test, and Abraham Lincoln himself did not make such a claim in the controversy over slavery before the Civil War.

The anti-slavery men at the Convention thought that they had won enough in these compromises to guarantee the slow decline and eventual end of slavery. They had seen it outlawed in some of their own states, and they looked forward to the abolition of the trade. Without importation of slaves, they thought, the free population would increase much faster than the slaves and it would become as possible for Georgia or South Carolina to abolish it as it had been for New York or Connecticut in their day. They thought that the limited land suitable for plantation agriculture, and the absence of slavery in the Northwest, together with its lack of respectability even in the South—men were unwilling to end it, but even more unwilling to praise it or deem it moral—would cause it to wither and die. Therefore, they accepted the compromises out of prudence, while they endeavored to sustain the founding principles, resolving to wait patiently in hope of the consummation of those principles.

THE CRISIS FACED BY LINCOLN

> ... [H]e who would be no slave, must consent to have no slave. Those who deny freedom to others, deserve it not for themselves; and, under a just God, cannot long retain it. All honor to Jefferson—to the man who, in the concrete pressure of a struggle for national independence by a single people, had the coolness, forecast, and capacity to introduce into a merely revolutionary document, an abstract truth, applicable to all men and all times, and so to embalm it there, that today, and in all coming days, it shall be a rebuke and a stumbling-block to the very harbingers of reappearing tyranny and oppression.
> – Abraham Lincoln, letter to Henry Pierce and others, April 6, 1859

Slavery did not wither and die in the generation after the founders. It was not enough to ban the importation of slaves; the American slave population, both African and Mulatto, grew naturally, and sons and daughters were cruelly torn from their families and sold to owners who set out to clear the lands of Alabama, Mississippi and the other Western territories where slavery was allowed. Breeding human beings made slavery economically efficient, and the cotton gin and other mechanical inventions made the plantation system profitable on lands that Madison and Jefferson thought would never be hospitable to slavery.

Slaves even began to be employed in the nascent manufacturing facilities of the South. The great Lincoln scholar, Harry Jaffa, cites the example of "a famous iron company in Richmond, Virginia, which introduced slaves into its labor force in the 1840's, with the result that the free laborers struck in protest." The manager broke the strike as managers sometimes do ... he would not rehire any of the strikers, and "[T]hereafter, the company employed only slaves."

In the North, parties and groups sprang up to resist slavery's expansion or to press for its abolition. In 1819–20, the proposal to admit Missouri to the Union was resisted by Northern Congressmen who demanded as a condition of their approval a plan for the gradual abolition of slavery in the newly admitted state. Madison wrote a friend that the debate gave him "no slight anxiety," and added that he saw nothing "to control those great repulsive Masses [sectional factions, based on the approval of slavery or its condemnation] from awful shocks against each other…." A famous letter of Jefferson's on the same subject declared, "... this momentous question, like a fire-bell in the night, awakened and filled me with terror. I considered it at once as the knell of the Union."

The failure of the policy of disapproval and patience, of voluntary manumission and non-importation, had made the issue a sectional question of the first magnitude. And worse, it began to produce sentiments like that of Calhoun quoted at the start of this section. Slavery apologist George Fitzhugh also explicitly rejected the moral sentiments of the previous generation of Southerners. Writing in 1857, he said that Southern writings of the previous generation "are like to be as absurd and as dangerous as the Declaration of Independence, or the Virginia Bill of Rights." Fitzhugh would have found nothing "absurd or dangerous" in what Alexander Stephens of Georgia would say in his famous "Cornerstone" speech at the March, 1861 Georgia convention called to ratify the Confederate Constitution:

> Our new government is founded upon exactly the opposite idea [namely, opposite to Jefferson's idea that slavery was wrong in principle]; its foundations are laid, its cornerstone rests upon the great truth, that the negro is not equal to the white man; that slavery—subordination to the superior race—is the normal condition…. This stone which was rejected by the first builders 'is become the chief of the corner'—the real 'cornerstone'—in our new edifice.

The quote within his quote is from Psalm 118:21. Stephens did not go on to add, "This is the Lord's doing, and it is marvelous in our eyes," but surely the text echoed in his hearers' minds as he spoke. Fighting words!

The Northern abolitionists were no less immoderate than these Southern proponents. The most prominent, William Lloyd Garrison, espoused secession of the North from the Union, and carried out public burnings of the Constitution, which Garrison called a "covenant with death."
Just consider these words from his journal, The Liberator:

> "I will be as harsh as truth, and as uncompromising as justice. On this subject, I do not wish to think, to speak, or write, with moderation.... I am in earnest—I will not equivocate—I will not excuse—I will not retreat a single inch—AND I WILL BE HEARD."

In this crisis of moral, political, and sectional strife, arose Abraham Lincoln.

CHAPTER 8

THE STATESMANSHIP OF ABRAHAM LINCOLN

> Four score and five years after the signing of the Declaration of Independence, the daring republican experiment consciously undertaken by the American Founding Fathers very nearly failed ignominiously, and it had to be revived by a man of even greater stature than Washington, Jefferson, Adams, Hamilton, and Madison—and at a cost in suffering and lives that seems staggering even in an epoch distinguished by mass murder and genocide. Abraham Lincoln's accomplishment was made even more wondrous by the fact that he anticipated the renewed need for grand statesmanship a quarter-century before he delivered the Gettysburg Address.
>
> – Paul Rahe, *Republics Ancient and Modern*, Volume III, page 231

Those who know principles are philosophers; those who know particulars are experts; those who bring them together are statesmen. The wisdom of the philosopher is made potent and the knowledge of the expert is made beneficial through the sagacity of the statesman. Statesmanship recollects the past, acts with wisdom in the present, and so fosters better things in the days to come. It requires experience, but it is more than experience. It knows the loves and the character of the political community that it shepherds, and it keeps that community faithful to what is good in its founding. In a few cases, statesmanship even elevates that founding. Statesmanship is rare.

American statesmanship, in its noblest moments, we will call "Declaration Statesmanship." We call it that because of what we have argued in earlier chapters, namely, that the Declaration is the American covenant, the public and written source of the principles that make the country what it is. Because we have such a founding document, together with a written constitution and similar "secular scripture," American statesmanship has a striking similarity to our religious heritage, Jewish and Christian. When we need national revival, we go back to the "book." Abraham Lincoln spoke in quintessentially American fashion when he said,

> I have never had a feeling politically that did not spring from the sentiments embodied in the Declaration of Independence ... I have often inquired of myself, what great principle or idea it was that kept this Confederacy so long together. It was not the mere matter of separation of the colonies from the mother land; but something in that Declaration giving liberty, not alone to the people of this country, but hope to the world for all future time. It was that which gave promise that in due time the weights would be lifted from the shoulders of all men, and that *all* should have an equal chance. This is the sentiment embodied in that Declaration of Independence.
>
> Now, my friends, can this country be saved upon that basis? If it can, I will consider myself one of the happiest men in the world if I can help to save it. If it can't be saved upon that principle, it will be truly awful. But if this country can't be saved without giving up that principle—I was about to say I would rather be assassinated on this spot than to surrender it.
>
> – Abraham Lincoln, *Speech*, Independence Hall, February 22, 1861

Lincoln, who spoke these words on his way to assume the duties of the Presidency, to which he had been elected that fall, showed another virtue of the statesman besides wisdom. Courage. He gave this speech, in public, having been warned of a plot to kill him.

But all this was in 1861. What does Paul Rahe mean in the text we cited at the beginning of this section, that Lincoln anticipated the need for "grand statesmanship" more than twenty years before this speech, when he was still a young man? Professor Rahe's reference is to a speech Lincoln gave in his home state of Illinois, in his hometown, Springfield, on January 27, 1838.

THE ADDRESS BEFORE THE YOUNG MEN'S LYCEUM OF SPRINGFIELD, ILLINOIS:

The Perpetuation of Our Political Institutions:

Address to the Young Men's Lyceum
Springfield, Illinois
Abraham Lincoln
January 27, 1838

As a subject for the remarks of the evening, the perpetuation of our political institutions, is selected.

In the great journal of things happening under the sun, we, the American People, find our account running, under date of the nineteenth century of the Christian era. We find ourselves in the peaceful possession, of the fairest portion of the earth, as regards extent of territory, fertility of soil, and salubrity of climate. We find ourselves under the government of a system of political institutions, conducing more essentially to the ends of civil and religious liberty, than any of which the history of former times tells us. We, when mounting the stage of existence, found ourselves the legal inheritors of these fundamental blessings. We toiled not in the acquirement or establishment of them—they are a legacy bequeathed us, by a once hardy, brave, and patriotic, but now lamented and departed race of ancestors. Their's was the task (and nobly they performed it) to possess themselves, and through themselves, us, of this goodly land; and to uprear upon its hills and its valleys, a political edifice of liberty and equal rights; 'tis ours only, to transmit these, the former, unprofaned by the foot of an invader; the latter, undecayed by the lapse of time, and untorn by usurpation—to the latest generation that fate shall permit the world to know. This task of gratitude to our fathers, justice to ourselves, duty to posterity, and love for our species in general, all imperatively require us faithfully to perform.

How, then, shall we perform it? At what point shall we expect the approach of danger? By what means shall we fortify against it? Shall we expect some transatlantic military giant, to step the Ocean, and crush us at a blow? Never! All the armies of Europe, Asia and Africa combined, with all the treasure of the earth (our own excepted) in their military chest; with a

Buonaparte for a commander, could not by force, take a drink from the Ohio, or make a track on the Blue Ridge, in a Trial of a thousand years.

At what point then is the approach of danger to be expected? I answer, if it ever reach us, it must spring up amongst us. It cannot come from abroad. If destruction be our lot, we must ourselves be its author and finisher. As a nation of freemen, we must live through all time, or die by suicide.

I hope I am over wary; but if I am not, there is, even now, something of ill-omen amongst us. I mean the increasing disregard for law which pervades the country; the growing disposition to substitute the wild and furious passions, in lieu of the sober judgement of Courts; and the worse than savage mobs, for the executive ministers of justice. This disposition is awfully fearful in any community; and that it now exists in ours, though grating to our feelings to admit, it would be a violation of truth, and an insult to our intelligence, to deny. Accounts of outrages committed by mobs, form the every-day news of the times. They have pervaded the country, from New England to Louisiana; — they are neither peculiar to the eternal snows of the former, nor the burning suns of the latter; — they are not the creature of climate — neither are they confined to the slaveholding, or the non-slaveholding States. Alike, they spring up among the pleasure hunting masters of Southern slaves, and the order loving citizens of the land of steady habits. Whatever, then, their cause may be, it is common to the whole country.

It would be tedious, as well as useless, to recount the horrors of all of them. Those happening in the State of Mississippi, and at St. Louis, are, perhaps, the most dangerous in example, and revolting to humanity. In the Mississippi case, they first commenced by hanging the regular gamblers: a set of men, certainly not following for a livelihood, a very useful, or very honest occupation; but one which, so far from being forbidden by the laws, was actually licensed by an act of the Legislature, passed but a single year before. Next, negroes, suspected of conspiring to raise an insurrection, were caught up and hanged in all parts of the State: then, white men, supposed to be leagued with the negroes; and finally, strangers, from neighboring States, going thither on business, were, in many instances, subjected to the same fate. Thus went on this process of hanging, from gamblers to negroes, from negroes to white citizens, and from these to strangers; till, dead men were seen literally dangling from the boughs of trees upon every road side; and in numbers almost sufficient, to rival the native Spanish moss of the country, as a drapery of the forest.

Turn, then, to that horror-striking scene at St. Louis. A single victim was only sacrificed there. His story is very short; and is, perhaps, the most highly tragic, of any thing of its length, that has ever been witnessed in real life. A mulatto man, by the name of McIntosh, was seized in the street, dragged to the suburbs of the city, chained to a tree, and actually burned to death; and all within a single hour from the time he had been a freeman, attending to his own business, and at peace with the world.

Such are the effects of mob law; and such are the scenes, becoming more and more frequent in this land so lately famed for love of law and order; and the stories of which, have even now grown too familiar, to attract any thing more, than an idle remark.

But you are, perhaps, ready to ask, "What has this to do with the perpetuation of our political institutions?" I answer, it has much to do with it. Its direct consequences are, comparatively speaking, but a small evil; and much of its danger consists, in the proneness of our minds, to regard its direct, as its only consequences. Abstractly considered, the hanging of the gamblers at Vicksburg, was of but little consequence. They constitute a portion of population, that is worse than useless in any community; and their death, if no pernicious example be set by it, is never matter of reasonable regret with any one. If they were annually swept, from the stage of existence, by the plague or small pox, honest men would, perhaps, be much profited, by the operation. Similar too, is the correct reasoning, in regard to the burning of the negro at St. Louis. He had forfeited his life, by the perpetration of an outrageous murder, upon one of the most worthy and respectable citizens of the city; and had he not died as he did, he must have died by the sentence of the law, in a very short time afterwards. As to him alone, it was as well the way it was, as it could otherwise have been. But the example in either case, was fearful. When men take it in their heads to day, to hang gamblers, or burn murderers, they should recollect, that, in the confusion usually attending such transactions, they will be as likely to hang or burn some one, who is neither a gambler nor a murderer as one who is; and that, acting upon the example they set, the mob of to-morrow, may, and probably will, hang or burn some of them, by the very same mistake. And not only so; the innocent, those who have ever set their faces against violations of law in every shape, alike with the guilty, fall victims to the ravages of mob law; and thus it goes on, step by step, till all the walls erected for the defence of the persons and property of individuals, are trodden down, and disregarded.

But all this even, is not the full extent of the evil. By such examples, by instances of the perpetrators of such acts going unpunished, the lawless in spirit, are encouraged to become lawless in practice; and having been used to no restraint, but dread of punishment, they thus become, absolutely unrestrained. Having ever regarded Government as their deadliest bane, they make a jubilee of the suspension of its operations; and pray for nothing so much, as its total annihilation. While, on the other hand, good men, men who love tranquility, who desire to abide by the laws, and enjoy their benefits, who would gladly spill their blood in the defence of their country; seeing their property destroyed; their families insulted, and their lives endangered; their persons injured; and seeing nothing in prospect that forebodes a change for the better; become tired of, and disgusted with, a Government that offers them no protection; and are not much averse to a change in which they imagine they have nothing to lose.

Thus, then, by the operation of this mobocratic spirit, which all must admit, is now abroad in the land, the strongest bulwark of any Government, and particularly of those constituted like ours, may effectually be broken down and destroyed — I mean the attachment of the People. Whenever this effect shall be produced among us; whenever the vicious portion of population shall be permitted to gather in bands of hundreds and thousands, and burn churches, ravage and rob provision stores, throw printing presses into rivers, shoot editors, and hang and burn obnoxious persons at pleasure, and with impunity; depend on it, this Government cannot last. By such things, the feelings of the best citizens will become more or less alienated from it; and thus it will be left without friends, or with too few, and those few too weak, to make their friendship effectual. At such a time and under such circumstances, men of sufficient talent and ambition will not be wanting to seize the opportunity, strike the blow, and overturn that fair fabric, which for the last half century, has been the fondest hope, of the lovers of freedom, throughout the world.

I know the American People are much attached to their Government; — I know they would suffer much for its sake; — I know they would endure evils long and patiently, before they would ever think of exchanging it for another. Yet, notwithstanding all this, if the laws be continually despised and disregarded, if their rights to be secure in their persons and property, are held by no better tenure than the caprice of a mob, the alienation of their affections from the Government is the natural consequence; and to that, sooner or later, it must come.

Here then, is one point at which danger may be expected.

The question recurs "how shall we fortify against it?" The answer is simple. Let every American, every lover of liberty, every well wisher to his posterity, swear by the blood of the Revolution, never to violate in the least particular, the laws of the country; and never to tolerate their violation by others. As the patriots of seventy-six did to the support of the Declaration of Independence, so to the support of the Constitution and Laws, let every American pledge his life, his property, and his sacred honor; — let every man remember that to violate the law, is to trample on the blood of his father, and to tear the character of his own, and his children's liberty. Let reverence for the laws, be breathed by every American mother, to the lisping babe, that prattles on her lap — let it be taught in schools, in seminaries, and in colleges; — let it be written in Primers, spelling books, and in Almanacs; — let it be preached from the pulpit, proclaimed in legislative halls, and enforced in courts of justice. And, in short, let it become the political religion of the nation; and let the old and the young, the rich and the poor, the grave and the gay, of all sexes and tongues, and colors and conditions, sacrifice unceasingly upon its altars.

While ever a state of feeling, such as this, shall universally, or even, very generally prevail throughout the nation, vain will be every effort, and fruitless every attempt, to subvert our national freedom.

When I so pressingly urge a strict observance of all the laws, let me not be understood as saying there are no bad laws, nor that grievances may not arise, for the redress of which, no legal provisions have been made. I mean to say no such thing. But I do mean to say, that, although bad laws, if they exist, should be repealed as soon as possible, still while they continue in force, for the sake of example, they should be religiously observed. So also in unprovided cases. If such arise, let proper legal provisions be made for them with the least possible delay; but, till then, let them if not too intolerable, be borne with.

There is no grievance that is a fit object of redress by mob law. In any case that arises, as for instance, the promulgation of abolitionism, one of two positions is necessarily true; that is, the thing is right within itself, and therefore deserves the protection of all law and all good citizens; or, it is wrong, and therefore proper to be prohibited by legal enactments; and in neither case, is the interposition of mob law, either necessary, justifiable, or excusable.

But, it may be asked, why suppose danger to our political institutions? Have we not preserved them for more than fifty years? And why may we not for fifty times as long?

We hope there is no sufficient reason. We hope all dangers may be overcome; but to conclude that no danger may ever arise, would itself be extremely dangerous. There are now, and will hereafter be, many causes, dangerous in their tendency, which have not existed heretofore; and which are not too insignificant to merit attention. That our government should have been maintained in its original form from its establishment until now, is not much to be wondered at. It had many props to support it through that period, which now are decayed, and crumbled away. Through that period, it was felt by all, to be an undecided experiment; now, it is understood to be a successful one. Then, all that sought celebrity and fame, and distinction, expected to find them in the success of that experiment. Their all was staked upon it: — their destiny was inseparably linked with it. Their ambition aspired to display before an admiring world, a practical demonstration of the truth of a proposition, which had hitherto been considered, at best no better, than problematical; namely, the capability of a people to govern themselves. If they succeeded, they were to be immortalized; their names were to be transferred to counties and cities, and rivers and mountains; and to be revered and sung, and toasted through all time. If they failed, they were to be called knaves and fools, and fanatics for a fleeting hour; then to sink and be forgotten. They succeeded.

The experiment is successful; and thousands have won their deathless names in making it so. But the game is caught; and I believe it is true, that with the catching, end the pleasures of the chase. This field of glory is harvested, and the crop is already appropriated. But new reapers will arise, and they, too, will seek a field. It is to deny, what the history of the world tells us is true, to suppose that men of ambition and talents will not continue to spring up amongst us. And, when they do, they will as naturally seek the gratification of their ruling passion, as others have so done before them. The question then, is, can that gratification be found in supporting and maintaining an edifice that has been erected by others? Most certainly it cannot. Many great and good men, sufficiently qualified for any task they should undertake, may ever be found, whose ambition would aspire to nothing beyond a seat in Congress, a gubernatorial or a presidential chair; but such belong not to the family of the lion, or the tribe of the eagle. What! think you these places would satisfy an Alexander, a Caesar, or a Napoleon? Never! Towering genius disdains a beaten path. It seeks regions hitherto unexplored. It sees no distinction in adding story to story, upon the monuments of fame, erected to the memory of others. It denies that it is glory enough to serve under any chief. It scorns to tread in the footsteps of any predecessor, however illustrious. It thirsts and burns for distinction; and, if possible, it will have it, whether at the expense of emancipating slaves, or enslaving freemen. Is it unreasonable then to expect, that some man possessed of the loftiest genius, coupled with ambition sufficient to push it to its utmost stretch, will at some time, spring up among us? And when such a one does, it will require the people to be united with each other, attached to the government and laws, and generally intelligent, to successfully frustrate his designs.

Distinction will be his paramount object; and although he would as willingly, perhaps more so, acquire it by doing good as harm; yet, that opportunity being past, and nothing left to be done in the way of building up, he would set boldly to the task of pulling down.

Here then, is a probable case, highly dangerous, and such a one as could not have well existed heretofore.

Another reason which once was; but which, to the same extent, is now no more, has done much in maintaining our institutions thus far. I mean the powerful influence which the interesting scenes of the revolution had upon the passions of the people as distinguished from their judgment. By this influence, the jealousy, envy, and avarice, incident to our nature, and so common to a state of peace, prosperity, and conscious strength, were, for the time, in a great measure smothered and rendered inactive; while the deep rooted principles of hate, and the powerful motive of revenge, instead of being turned against each other, were directed exclusively against the British nation. And thus, from the force of circumstances, the basest principles of our nature, were either made to lie dormant, or to become the active agents in the advancement of the noblest of causes — that of establishing and maintaining civil and religious liberty.

But this state of feeling must fade, is fading, has faded, with the circumstances that produced it.

I do not mean to say, that the scenes of the revolution are now or ever will be entirely forgotten; but that like every thing else, they must fade upon the memory of the world, and grow more and more dim by the lapse of time. In history, we hope, they will be read of, and recounted, so long as the bible shall be read; — but even granting that they will, their influence cannot be what it heretofore has been. Even then, they cannot be so universally known, nor so vividly felt, as they were by the generation just gone to rest. At the close of that struggle, nearly every adult male had been a participator in some of its scenes. The consequence was, that of those scenes, in the form of a husband, a father, a son or a brother, a living history was to be found in every family — a history bearing the indubitable testimonies of its own authenticity, in the limbs mangled, in the scars of wounds received, in the midst of the very scenes related — a history, too, that could be read and understood alike by all, the wise and the ignorant, the learned and the unlearned. But those histories are gone. They can be read no more forever. They were a fortress of strength; but, what invading foemen could never do, the silent artillery of time has done; the levelling of its walls. They are gone. They were a forest of giant oaks; but the all resistless hurricane has swept over them, and left only, here and there, a lonely trunk, despoiled of its verdure, shorn of its foliage; unshading and unshaded, to murmur in a few more gentle breezes, and to combat with its mutilated limbs, a few more ruder storms, then to sink, and be no more.

They were the pillars of the temple of liberty; and now, that they have crumbled away, that temple must fall, unless we, their descendants, supply their places with other pillars, hewn from the solid quarry of sober reason. Passion has helped us; but can do so no more. It will in future be our enemy. Reason, cold, calculating, unimpassioned reason, must furnish all the materials for our future support and defence. Let those materials be moulded into general intelligence, sound morality and, in particular, a reverence for the constitution and laws; and, that we improved to the last; that we remained free to the last; that we revered his name to the last; that, during his long sleep, we permitted no hostile foot to pass over or desecrate his resting place; shall be that which to learn the last trump shall awaken our WASHINGTON.

Upon these let the proud fabric of freedom rest, as the rock of its basis; and as truly as has been said of the only greater institution, "the gates of hell shall not prevail against it."

We will make a few remarks in the way of analysis of this speech, but first, to give a word of praise to our forefathers, who cared enough for reason and civic life that they could and did spend their precious leisure hours meeting to listen to speeches like this. The Young Men's Lyceum was a kind of civic and educational society that sponsored events like the one featuring the gangly young hometown lawyer's speech on "the perpetuation of our political institutions." One of the ways to perpetuate our liberties, to perform what Lincoln called "this task of gratitude" is to use our minds in understanding and hence cherishing our "legacy," our republican inheritance. Life was rough in Springfield in 1838, but even on the frontier, tired men found time and energy to devote to the art of being free.

One bit of fact that underlies the speech is noteworthy. About ten weeks before Lincoln spoke in Springfield, not sixty miles away, in Alton, Illinois, an armed mob had shot and killed a newspaper editor, Elijah P. Lovejoy. Mr. Lovejoy, an abolitionist and also anti-Catholic agitator, had castigated the people and authorities in Missouri for the lynching so vividly described in the earlier part of the speech. Three times his presses had been thrown into the Mississippi; he died, gun in hand, defending a newly purchased fourth press. Lincoln acknowledges these events in passing, in the words, "throw printing-presses into rivers, shoot editors." The connection between the Lovejoy episode and the Negro murdered in St. Louis means that race, slavery, and abolitionism lurked in the background, though, it should be stressed, the background only, of Lincoln's account of the dangers that violence and passion posed to American institutions.

We now give a somewhat oversimplified sketch of the plan of the speech:

I. Introduction and theme: the task of perpetuation
II. Three dangers and their remedies
    A. Mob rule, either from passion or from idealist extremism, and its remedy, reverence for the laws
    B. Great ambition in great men, provoked by the once-for-all character of the founding, and a partial remedy, resistance by a united people
    C. Weak attachment to the founding, due to the passing away of the revolutionary generation, and to dimming memory, and the consequent increase in the danger posed by the passions of the people and its remedy, sober reason
III. Conclusion, comparison of the American republic to the church, and the implied marriage of reason and reverence

What may be seen about Lincoln's purpose, his statesmanship, in this speech? In a way, everything is implied in its theme: *on the perpetuation of our political institutions.* Lincoln saw that the revolutionary generation was dying, and with it the living memory of the fight for the principles of the Declaration. He saw too that the experiment had been so far a success, with the exception of the continuation and spread of slavery. In particular, he saw that the blessings of liberty implied prosperity and comfort, and a consequent decline in the noble ambitions and spirit of sacrifice that made the founding possible. In the vigilante justice of his day, he saw a tendency for the "old Adam," the man of selfish and violent passions, to resurface. This is a permanent danger. Just think of the rioters who have blocked reputable speakers from being heard on college campuses and terrorized the streets of Portland and other cities. And yet, in our own day, we note in passing, coldness of soul, sloth, and indifference might undermine the laws even more than the heat and malevolence that leads to riots.

The Declaration had asserted self-evident truths. That meant, as we have said in earlier chapters, truths accessible to and sometimes held only by reason. These truths are mightily bolstered by religious faith, but not all men are believers, and not all believers are equally fervent and faithful throughout their lives. Declaration principles, the creed of the founders, had been upheld by *feelings* not to be counted on long beyond the lives of the original patriots. As the text runs:

> But this state of feeling *must fade, is fading, has faded,* with the circumstances that produced it.

Lincoln gives as the remedy for this fading, in his account of the third danger, "sober reason." But his words there can be misleading. For he had urged earlier that "as the patriots of seventy-six did to the support of the Declaration," so now Americans of later generations should to the laws and Constitution, pledge, life, property, and "sacred honor." He urges mothers, teachers, preachers, politicians— all Americans— to have and inculcate "reverence for the laws," and he concludes this section, which deals with the first danger, mob violence, whether of vigilantes, or of bigots, or of abolitionists, by prescribing as remedy reverence for the laws. But he calls this reverence, not "reason," but "a state of feeling."

We may say, then, that Lincoln's prescription for the health of the American body politic is to provide a shield against the eternal dangers posed by the passions, a shield of reason fortified with an almost religious reverence for the spirit and letter of the laws. But he does not make an Idol of Law.

Like St. Paul, he places the spirit over the letter, since, as he freely acknowledges, the letter can be in error:

> Let me not be understood as saying there are no bad laws, or that grievances may not arise for the redress of which, no legal provisions have been made. I mean to say no such thing." Bad laws are not to be idolized, they are to be changed, and in the meantime, unless they are intolerable, to be obeyed, "for the sake of example."

Lincoln's forceful admonition that Americans be habituated to "reverence for the laws" has been characterized as "Civic Religion," and criticized by some believers as verging on idolatry. Perhaps there are dangers in that direction, but the language of devotion is traditional in American political discourse. Here is a nice instance from Calvin Coolidge. Note the use of the word "faithfully."

> These principles of independence, of the integrity of the Union, and of local self-government have not diminished in their importance since they were so clearly recognized and faithfully declared in the Virginia convention of 150 years ago. We may wonder at their need of constant restatement, reiteration, and defense. But the fact is that the principles of government have the same need to be fortified, reinforced, and supported that characterize the principles of religion. After enumerating many of the spiritual ideals, the Scriptures enjoin us to 'think on these things.' If we are to maintain the ideals of government, it is likewise necessary that we 'think on these things.' It is for this purpose that educational institutions exist, and important anniversaries are observed.
> – President Coolidge, *Commemorative Address given on the 150th Anniversary of the Virginia Resolutions of 1776*

Lincoln had been reading *The Federalist* in the period before he gave this speech. Perhaps his thought was provoked by the passage below. Note the exact expression, used by Lincoln in 1838, "reverence for the laws."

> The reason of man, like man himself, is timid and cautious when left alone, and acquires firmness and confidence in proportion to the number with which it is associated. When the examples which fortify opinion are *ancient* as well as *numerous*, they are known to have a double effect. In a nation of philosophers, this consideration ought to be disregarded. A reverence for the laws would be sufficiently inculcated by the voice of enlightened reason. But a nation of philosophers is as little to be expected as the philosophical race of kings wished for by Plato. And in every other nation, the most rational government will not find it a superfluous advantage to have the prejudices of the community on its side.
> – *Federalist 49*

Lincoln's project, the work for which he finally gave the last, full measure of devotion, was to ennoble these "prejudices," filling them with reason, morality, and a feeling of reverence for the rule of law and for the principles of eternal right enshrined in the founding.

That is how he dedicated himself to perpetuate our political institutions.

THE SECOND DANGER AND THE GREAT MAN

Lincoln says nothing about a *self-imposed* remedy for the danger posed by the great man, for him of the "family of the lion, or the tribe of the eagle." He almost seems to be warning *himself* about this danger, when he goes on to say of such a genius, "It thirsts and burns for distinction; and, if possible, it will have it, whether at the expense of emancipating slaves, or enslaving freemen." Perhaps he means to leave reflection on this danger to similar souls, and gives only a glimpse of it here, to the rest of us. Perhaps this great man will find his satisfaction in the work that history gives him, to revive and re-establish a nation with a noble founding, a work whose need will arise whenever men forget their high calling under the laws of nature and nature's God, and devote themselves to mere interest, comfort, and private gain.

FROM THE REPEAL OF THE MISSOURI COMPROMISE TO THE PRESIDENCY

> ... In 1846 I was once elected to the lower House of Congress. Was not a candidate for re-election. From 1849 to 1854, both inclusive, practiced law more assiduously than ever before. Always a whig in politics, and generally on the whig electoral tickets, making active canvasses. I was losing interest in politics, when the repeal of the Missouri Compromise aroused me again. What I have done since then is pretty well known.
> – Abraham Lincoln, from a letter to Jesse W. Fell, as material for a campaign biography, December 20, 1859

The Missouri Compromise is the name commonly used for a number of legislative and political acts taken in 1820, chief among which were the admission of two states to the Union, Missouri and Maine, and the prohibition of slavery in the portion of the Louisiana purchase north of the line of latitude 36' 30", approximately the southern boundary of the state of Missouri. The debate on the question of Missouri's admission as a slave state had been bitter and sectional. In the House, where they had a numerical advantage of 105–81, the representatives of the North voted almost unanimously for a phased-in prohibition of slavery. The Senate, however, where the numbers of Southern and Northern Senators were equal, consistently blocked this prohibition. John Quincy Adams, Madison, and Jefferson were all aghast at the stark sectionalism of the vote, and Jefferson's remark, quoted in Chapter 7, above, that it was "like a fire-bell in the night," has become famous. Adams, who was then Secretary of State, wrote in his diary that, "If the Union must be dissolved, slavery is precisely the question upon which it ought to break."

The struggle over Missouri did not appear to all the men of the day as altogether about the morality or justice of slavery. The new Western lands, and the natural increase of the slave population, augmented by legal importation before 1808, and by slave smuggling after then, had kept the

South a region of agriculture, and with the invention of the cotton gin, an agriculture that included a significant portion of profitable, large scale, slave labor operations. The 'advanced' farmers of the South, and certainly the wealthiest of them, found in slaves the chief source of their labor force. The agricultural and slave-owning interest also constituted a commercial faction opposed to tariffs. Tariffs were import taxes on foreign goods, mostly manufactures. The infant Northern manufacturing interest sought tariffs to protect itself against European, and especially English, competition. A Missouri with slavery would presumably also be a state whose representatives would support Southern, agrarian, and anti-tariff policies in future Congresses. When the Missouri question arose, the Senate had exactly the same number of free states and slave states, eleven. Maine's desire for admission as a separate state (it had hitherto been a portion of Massachusetts) gave both parties a way out of the standoff.

The opponents of slavery obtained the prohibition north of the 36' 30" line, an extension of the policy of the founders in the Northwest Ordinance, which had contained a similar provision. Maine was admitted as a free state in 1820, and Missouri was admitted as a slave state in 1821, though it had to accept a second compromise, demanded by Henry Clay, to recognize the constitutional rights of Negro citizens of the United States.

Almost all of the remaining territory owned by the United States at that time (the sole exception was the portion of the Louisiana Purchase that was to become the state of Arkansas; Florida was not acquired until 1821) was thus under a federal ban against slavery. This put into the national law an obstacle to further growth of slavery, much as the Ordinance of 1787 had, and it reaffirmed the moral principle behind that ordinance. It is also reaffirmed the right of Congress to legislate about slavery and everything else in United States' *territories.*

The three chief goods of the compromise, as they appeared to Lincoln, were these: the ensuring that territory north of the Line would be free, the right of Congress so to act, and the moral disapprobation of slavery effected through its having so acted.

THE COMPROMISE HOLDS: 1821-1854

We now compress our story even further. In this period of Western expansion, the states formed out of the old Northwest Territory or above 36' 30" came in as free states: Michigan in 1837 through Minnesota in 1858. Arkansas, below the line, entered with slavery in 1836, and Florida in 1845. Texas, after a period of independence, came in with slavery in 1845. The boundary disputes between Texas, now an American state, and Mexico, culminating in the Mexican-American War, gave rise to new disputes over the prohibition of slavery in any territory to be acquired from Mexico. As in the Missouri controversy, Congress was split by section and between the two houses. Lincoln, who was in the House of Representatives, consistently voted with the majority for the prohibition, which was called the Wilmot Proviso (after its author, a Democrat from Pennsylvania). The Senate, in which the South had a larger share of the members, consistently rejected the Wilmot Proviso.

The Missouri Compromise had not granted those favoring extension of slavery the right to have it in federal territory *south* of the 36' 30" line; it had only banned slavery *north* of it. Hence, Lincoln and the "Proviso men" resisted a motion by Senator Douglas to extend the line to the Pacific Ocean. It would have cut California, which was filling up with gold miners and other immigrants, and already seeking admission to the union in 1849, into two regions. They feared that one would produce a state with slavery and the other, one without it, and they wanted the whole of California free. California, like Texas, had been an independent republic. Its request for admission to the union was blocked in the Senate because the inhabitants wished to come in with a prohibition of slavery.

The California question headed a list of slavery related matters that were resolved in the Compromise of 1850. As with the Missouri Compromise, each side gave something. The North yielded on a fugitive slave law and certain payments to Texas. The South accepted California as a free state and let restrictions be placed on the slave market in the District of Columbia. Utah and New Mexico were allowed to choose to enter the Union, at some later date, as slave or free, but no concession was made limiting the federal power to govern them while they were territories. Most of the leading politicians declared themselves tolerably well satisfied with these arrangements, and both major parties, at that time the Whigs and the Democrats, endorsed it in their national conventions.

Throughout this thirty-year period, among the people, the deeper questions smoldered and sometimes flared. Direct denunciations of the equality taught by the Declaration began to be heard from apologists for slavery, while abolitionists like the doomed Lovejoy made equally fierce attacks on the Constitution. Small but frightening slave rebellions, few in number, but big with terror, prompted Southern states to patrol the roads at night for black men breaking curfew, and to prohibit the teaching of reading and writing to slaves, lest they should catch a contagion of liberty from Northern abolitionists. The great Protestant denominations, Methodists, Baptists, and Presbyterians, began to divide on sectional lines. Sentiment in the lower south, the "Cotton Kingdom" was clearly shifting from toleration of slavery as a perplexing and troublesome evil to defense of it as a positive good.

These underlying differences were not settled by the Compromise. In some respects they may have been worsened. Bitterness over the obligation to obey the hated fugitive slave law fueled defiance and sometimes non-compliance in the New England states. Indeed, as prominent a man as Ralph Waldo Emerson advised his fellow citizens to break it "on the earliest possible occasion." Confiding to his diary, he was yet more strident:

> This filthy enactment was made in the nineteenth century, by people who could read and write.I will not obey it, by God!
> – *Emerson: The Mind on Fire*, by Robert Richardson, Jr., p. 498

It was the fugitive slave law that set Harriet Beecher Stowe to writing *Uncle Tom's Cabin*, one of the most incendiary novels of all time. It was a Northern and an international sensation, translated into twenty languages and selling over a million copies in the first couple of years after its publication. The dramatic depiction of the cruel slave master and his suffering slaves infuriated the more humane slave owners who knew how it caricatured their own practice. Forgotten, perhaps, or overlooked, was how much of it was true. The passionate reaction of slavery apologists culminated in the defiant writings of George Fitzhugh, whose polemics included statements like,

> The negro slaves of the South are the happiest, and in some sense, the freest people in the world....

and,

> ... the whole literature of free society is but a voice proclaiming its absolute and total failure. [Fitzhugh has in mind here the scandals of child labor, and the discarded and poor elderly, discussed and lamented in the liberal and Northern press.] Hence the works of the socialists contain the true defence of slavery.
> – *Cannibals All*, George Fitzhugh, 1857

It is hard to know what the leaders who had worked out the Compromise of 1850 would have thought of these deep fault lines. They were among the great names of American history: Webster, Clay, Calhoun, Stephen Douglas, Jefferson Davis, and Seward. The first three were all dead within two years of the agreement, and the last two found themselves on opposite sides of the Civil War a dozen years later. Senator Douglas would soon act to end the ban on slavery north of the 36' 30" line, a key element of the Compromise, taking an action that he knew would raise a terrific a storm. But this would not happen until 1854. In 1850, the nation's leaders had avoided open schism, and the lovers of the Union continued to live in hope.

Congressman Lincoln, whose popularity had declined in his house district because he had raised objections to the war of conquest in Mexico, did not run for re-election to the House. He returned to Illinois, and gave himself to the practice of law.

POPULAR SOVEREIGNTY AND STEPHEN A. DOUGLAS

> I regard the great principle of popular sovereignty, as having been vindicated and made triumphant in this land, as a permanent rule of public policy in the organization of Territories and the admission of new States....
>
> I deny their [Congress'] right to force a good thing upon a people who are unwilling to receive it. The great principle is the right of every community to judge and decide of itself, whether a thing is right or wrong, whether it would be good or evil for them to adopt it; and the right of free action, the right of free thought, the right of free judgement upon the question is dearer to every true American than any other under a free government.
> – Stephen A. Douglas, Speech, Chicago Illinois, July, 9, 1858

> The North has only to will it [the saving of the Union] to accomplish it; to do justice by conceding to the South an equal right in the acquired territory, and to do her duty by causing the stipulations relative to the fugitive slaves to be faithfully fulfilled; to *cease the agitation of the slavery question....*
> – John C. Calhoun, Speech to the Senate, March 4, 1850 [italics added]

As we saw above, Lincoln wrote in his sketch for his Presidential campaign biography that, "the repeal of the Missouri Compromise aroused me again." Draft language of that repeal was announced in a Washington newspaper in mid-January of 1854 as follows:

> [an amendment will be added to the Nebraska bill stipulating that] the Constitution, and all laws of the United States which are not locally inapplicable, shall have the same force and effect within the said Territory of Nebraska as elsewhere within the United States, *except the eighth section of the act preparatory to the Admission of Missouri into the Union, approved March 6, 1820, which was superseded by the principles of the legislation of 1850, commonly called the compromise measures, and is hereby declared inoperative.*

Senator Stephen A. Douglas of Illinois was the Chairman of the Senate Committee on Territories; Douglas consented to the amendment, and the bill passed. This meant that the federal ban on slavery in the Territory, which was divided into a southern portion, the Kansas Territory, and a northern, the Nebraska Territory, was void. As Douglas had predicted, a terrific storm arose.

What did Douglas intend? There can be no doubt that he wanted the Union to survive and prosper. Moreover, he was not, like Calhoun, of the "slavery as a positive good" school. Indeed, Douglas had supported the admission of California as a free state, and the organization of the Oregon Territory, in which Congress adopted an amendment authored by Douglas recognizing the existing ban on slavery, enacted by the settlers themselves.

Douglas was an intelligent and bold politician, ambitious for the Presidency. He would be the candidate of the Northern Democrats in 1860, running against Lincoln. He saw the threat of disunion, and he had heard the resentment in his Southern Democratic colleagues like Calhoun. Calhoun had all but demanded that no one even talk about slavery as a political question. That is what he meant in saying that the North could bring an end to the threat of disunion by ceasing to "agitate" the issue of slavery. Douglas sought a bold answer to the Union's troubles. It would require practical politics and principle. He called his answer "Popular Sovereignty."

As a policy, "Popular Sovereignty" meant that Congress would no longer prohibit slavery in any United States' territories. The question would be handed over to the people of the territories as they organized themselves. It would be addressed again in their conventions when they grew ripe for statehood. Since the fugitive slave law was now in effect, and since the overseas slave trade had been illegal for nearly fifty years, this meant that there should be no reason for any discussion or "agitation" on the issue to arise in Congress again. He further promised not to "care" about what the people of any territory seeking admission had decided on the issue in preparing for admission as a state, so long as they had done it fairly.

This was meant to satisfy the demands of Calhoun's heirs in the South. The national argument, as a political argument, was to cease, because the issue, as some say now about abortion, "didn't belong in politics." But on the question of the spread of slavery, Douglas's solution had some appeal to the North, since many thought it unlikely that the northern climate would be hospitable to the plantation agriculture, chiefly cotton and rice, that had been home to slavery in the South. If this hunch about the economics of the spread of slavery were true, then the Union would become progressively more and more dominated by free states, without anyone having to raise the question of the morality of slavery, and thereby offending the slave interest in the South.

To make all this work, Douglas had to persuade his fellow Americans that "Popular Sovereignty" was the cornerstone of the republic. He had some reason to think that it was, and that he could make a majority think so. For one thing, the principle squared with the American fondness for local control. Douglas would point out in his 1858 debates with Lincoln that liquor laws, and agricultural laws, and a host of other ordinances differed from Maine to Louisiana, and that we liked it that way. Jefferson himself had been a strong proponent of states' rights and of local self-government. At the same time, within these local communities, the will of the people had been held sovereign. Jefferson had called the rule of the will of the majority a "sacred principle" in his First Inaugural Address.

But there were problems with Douglas's formulation. He might say, "I don't care," about local decisions on slavery, but people *did* care. In the case of Kansas, they would care enough to send armed bodies of settlers to inflate the votes of their side in the territorial disputes on the way to statehood. These men cared enough to shed blood over the question. It was not perfectly evident that slavery could only prove profitable growing cash crops in warm climates; we noticed above that in Richmond a successful factory enterprise employed slave labor exclusively. In our century, countries like China have made effective, if inhumane, use of slaves, as did the old Soviet Union, in very cold climates. Poor workers, especially "guest workers" and illegal immigrants, not to mention innocent and poor young women and children, can find themselves in conditions similar to slavery even at present, in all kinds of climates and in various "walks of life." Slavery, *de jure*, and *de facto*, is an endemic disease among mankind, alas!

Moreover, it was not clear when Douglas was setting forth popular sovereignty in the 1850's whether the slaveholding settlers who would share in deciding the question would bring their slaves with them, and, if they did, whether they would have the benefit of laws to protect their 'property.' If they did, slavery would be established *de facto* before any vote on it. Most important of all, popular sovereignty, in its fundamental sense, majority rule, is not a complete statement of the American Creed. Jefferson's exact words, from his inaugural address, in which he called the popular will "sacred," deserve quotation in full:

> All, too, will bear in mind this sacred principle, that though the will of the majority is in all cases to prevail, that will to be rightful must be reasonable; that the minority possess their equal rights, which equal law must protect, and to violate would be oppression.
> – Thomas Jefferson, *First Inaugural*, March 4, 1801

Douglas's policy and that of the founders were alike in key points, but different in others. Both thought that the preservation of the Union was paramount. Both agreed in refusing to interfere with slavery where it existed. Both looked to a change to be produced by time and patience. But the founders had used the power of Congress to block the expansion of slavery and to strengthen the conviction that it was wrong. Douglas looked to popular sovereignty to produce the first effect while he took affirmative action to see that the second, the conviction that it was wrong, would not be expressed in the public arena. This meant that he differed from the founders in principle, and not only in policy. Douglas had made self-rule, and not self-evident truths, the deepest principle of free government. Lincoln thought the policy harmful; he was convinced that the principle, as Douglas's understanding would have it, was false. That is what "aroused" him in 1854.

LINCOLN AROUSED: THE PEORIA SPEECH

> The doctrine of self-government is right—absolutely and eternally right—but it has no just application as here attempted. Or perhaps I should rather say that whether it has such application depends on whether a negro is *not* or *is* a man. If he is *not* a man, why in that case, he who *is* a man may, as a matter of self-government, do just as he pleases with him. But if the negro *is* a man, is it not to just that extent a total destruction of self-government, to say that he too shall not govern *himself*? When the white man governs himself that is self-government; but when he governs himself, and also governs *another* man, that is *more* than self-government—that is despotism. If the negro is a *man,* why then my ancient faith teaches me that "all men are created equal;" and that there can be no moral right in connection with one man's making a slave of another.
>
> Judge Douglas frequently, with bitter irony and sarcasm, paraphrases our argument by saying: "the white people of Nebraska are good enough to govern themselves, *but they are not good enough to govern a few miserable negros!!*"
>
> Well I doubt not that the people of Nebraska are, and will continue to be as good as the average of people elsewhere. I do not say the contrary. What I do say is, that no man is good enough to govern another man *without that other's consent.* I say

> that this is the leading principle—the sheet anchor of American republicanism.
>
> – Abraham Lincoln, *Speech*, Peoria, Illinois, October 16, 1854

Lincoln's Peoria speech merits our attention for several powerful reasons. It was an immediate success in its day. It is carefully researched. And it gives the heart of his disagreement with Douglas on facts, policy, and principles.

Lincoln gave essentially the same speech at least four times, writing out the second, the one given in Peoria, for publication in the *Illinois State Journal*. Lincoln had asked Douglas to have the Peoria event be a debate; Douglas told a friend that he didn't want to debate Lincoln, saying "[he is] ... the most difficult and dangerous opponent that I have ever met." Instead of holding a debate, they spoke one after another to the same crowd, Douglas going first. Lincoln's shrewd political sense manifested itself in the timing; he told the tired crowd to go have dinner and come back before hearing him. Douglas had worn them out with a three hour address on a warm afternoon! To make sure they returned, he also offered Douglas an hour's rebuttal to "skin me."

The opening sentence gives the subject of the speech in plain, homespun simplicity: "The repeal of the Missouri compromise, and the propriety of its restoration, constitute the subject of what I am about to say." The first quarter or so is a thorough review of the policy of Congress regarding slavery from the time of the Articles of Confederation down to the present day. We have summarized that history above. It establishes conclusively that Congresses from before the Constitution up to the 1850's held that they had the power to restrict slavery in national territories, and had often used that power.

STATESMANSHIP: Fidelity to Principles

The heart of the speech is Lincoln's treatment of the contradiction between popular sovereignty as applied to slavery, and natural right as enshrined in the Declaration. If anyone, black, white, yellow, or brown, is a man, and if I arrogate to myself, and to men of my race only, the right to choose whether that man and his kind shall be slaves or not, I cannot have grounded that decision in the *universal* proposition that "all men are created equal" and hence "endowed by their creator with certain unalienable rights."

Since I am no longer measured, that is, held to a moral measure, in my choice, how shall I make it? Douglas's understanding of popular sovereignty comes to saying that the "sacred right of self-government" allows a moral right in one man's enslaving another. Lincoln says that the real meaning of Douglas doctrine would lead men "into an open war with the very principles of civil liberty—criticizing the Declaration of Independence, and insisting that there is no right principle of action but *self-interest.*"

Indeed, not only *would* the popular sovereignty basis of the Nebraska Bill lead men to disparage the Declaration, it had already done so, and not only the chieftains of the slave power, like Calhoun. The eloquence of the following passage from the Peoria speech demands that it be quoted at length:

> Little by little, but steadily as man's march to the grave, we have been giving up the OLD for the NEW faith. Near eighty years ago we began by declaring that all men are created equal; but now from that beginning we have run down to the other declaration, that for SOME men to enslave OTHERS is a "sacred right of self-government." These principles cannot stand together. They are as opposite as God and mammon; and whoever holds to the one, must despise the other.
>
> When Pettit [Senator from Indiana], in connection with his support of the Nebraska bill, called the Declaration of Independence "a self-evident lie," he only did what consistency and candor require all other Nebraska men to do. Of the forty odd Nebraska Senators who sat present and heard him, no one rebuked him. Nor am I apprized that any Nebraska newspaper, or any Nebraska orator, in the whole nation, has ever yet rebuked him. If this had been said among [Francis] Marion's men, Southerners though they were, what would have become of the man who said it? If this had been said to the men who captured [Major] Andre, the man who said it, would probably have been hung sooner than Andre was. If it had been said in old Independence Hall, seventy-eight years ago, the very door-keeper would have throttled the man, and thrust him into the street.

STATESMANSHIP: Our Place in History

Americans had, and have, a special duty because we have natural rights spelled out in our founding "scripture." Our British brethren, against whom we had written the Declaration, abolished slavery in 1832 because they felt themselves measured by the standard of human equality and Christian morality. So had the newly liberated South American Republics. Brazil, a self-styled "Empire," kept slavery until 1888. The next year it became a republic and abolished it.

It may have been fairly easy for the British to end slavery, given that there was none of it in the home island, and Spanish Latin America did not have as extensive or as regional a slave establishment as did the United States. Still, they had cleansed themselves of this evil, and we had not. Our reputation, our prestige, was at issue. Lincoln was not alone in feeling ashamed at our loss of moral leadership, and he said so in the speech:

> I hate it [Douglas's declared 'indifference' to slavery] because of the monstrous injustice of slavery itself. I hate it because it deprives our republican example of its just influence in the world—enables the enemies of free institutions, with plausibility, to taunt us as hypocrites—causes the real friends of freedom to doubt our sincerity....

The thought that America has a special duty to mankind to vindicate republican government was, of course, not original with Lincoln. We have already seen that it was prominent in *Federalist* 1. If the young republic failed, it would be, according to Publius,"the general misfortune of mankind." Washington told his fellow citizens, in his First Inaugural Address,

> ... the preservation of the sacred fire of liberty and the destiny of the republican model of government are justly considered, perhaps, as *deeply*, as *finally*, staked on the experiment intrusted to the hands of the American people.

In the 20th century, Presidents Eisenhower and Kennedy, among others, have spoken along the same lines regarding the scandal of race discrimination.

Here is Eisenhower, addressing a national television audience in response to the defiance of Arkansas state authority to the desegregation of Central High School in Little Rock:

> At a time when we face grave situations abroad because of the hatred that Communism bears towards a system of government based on human rights, it would be difficult to exaggerate the harm that is being done to [our] prestige and influence....

Or Kennedy in 1963:

> ... [racial discrimination] hampers our world leadership by contradicting at home the message we preach abroad.

It is interesting that both of these recent presidents cited the Declaration in their inaugural addresses. In making the charge that he did, that Douglas' 'Popular Sovereignty' doctrine and his 'don't care' posture "deprive ... our ... example of its just influence...." Lincoln showed the breadth of vision and the goodwill, as well as the attitude of a wise servant, that characterizes high statesmanship.

STATESMANSHIP: Opinion, the Material of the Statesman, and Words, his Instrument

As we read the Peoria speech today, one element jars our sensibilities: Lincoln does not take a stand for full political and social equality of the races. Some of the abolitionists of his day, especially the Quakers and other religious abolitionists, did. The 1854 laws of Maine set up in almost all respects what we would recognize today as equal civil rights, including jury duty and voting rights. But Maine was almost alone. Illinois' laws did not allow blacks to vote or serve on juries, and Illinois was typical of the free states.

In Peoria, Lincoln said this: "Let it not be said that I am contending for the establishment of political and social equality between the whites and blacks. I have already said the contrary." Was this statesmanlike too, or was it either weak or unwise, or even unjust?

> I think Lincoln's position in the Peoria speech can be vindicated, and that it can be reconciled with his support for

> expanded civil rights towards the end of the Civil War, if two things are kept in mind. First, as Lincoln himself said in 1859, "In this country, public opinion is everything." Second, that the knowledge of the statesman is prudence, or practical wisdom, which consists in knowing how to move towards moral goals by practicable steps, not in "the immoderate pursuit of moral perfection" which, in political life, "will more often lead to misery and terror than to justice and happiness," as Thomas G. West puts it in his book, *Vindicating the Founders.*

To begin with the first point, is it not self-evident that in a republic, where the citizens are governed by their consent, their opinion will be the court of last resort, the final arbiter of all disputes? That does not mean that those opinions will never change, or that it will not be the duty of a good man and especially of a statesman to mold them for the better. But a public man will ignore them at his peril. Lincoln turns this weapon back on Douglas in the Peoria speech, when he tells him that he will never be able to suppress the voice of the people crying out that slavery is unjust: "... the great mass of mankind ... consider slavery a great moral wrong; and their feeling against it, is not evanescent, but eternal. It lies at the very foundation of their sense of justice; and it cannot be trifled with—It is a great and durable element of popular action, and I think, no statesman can safely disregard it."

Sir Francis Bacon wrote long ago that, "Nature, to be mastered, must be obeyed." The saying is equally true of the nature of the physical body and of the body politic. Public opinion, the soul of the political body, was ailing in the days after the Nebraska Bill, and Douglas was prescribing as medicine what Lincoln thought poison. That the patient should also take up a regimen of vigorous exercise after his recovery was not and should not have been the first thing on the doctor's list.

Lincoln never said that political equality between the races was wrong; the most complete expression of his early views on the matter came in the 1858 debates with Douglas, and he clothed them entirely in the language of feeling:

> ... [I said years ago[11] that] my own feelings would not admit a social and political equality between the black and white races, and that even if my own feelings would admit of it, I still knew that the public sentiment of the country would not, and that such a thing was an utter impossibility, or substantially that.

And again, in the same debate,

> I agree with Judge Douglas that he [the Negro] is not my equal in many respects, certainly not in color— *perhaps* not in intellectual and moral endowments; but in the right to eat the bread without the leave of any body else which his own hand earns, he is my equal and the equal of Judge Douglas, and the equal of every other man.

It must be remembered that the young Lincoln had said in 1838 that our passions, our feelings, were to be the enemy of our freedom in the future, and that reason, "cold sober reason," would be the friend of the principles of the Declaration. Only one feeling, an almost religious reverence for the founding ideals, would buttress that reason. It should also be pointed out that Lincoln said that he knew only that the *feelings* of his fellow citizens would not admit of equality. He was certain that there was an inequality of "color." He did *not* say that he was certain of the infinitely more important inequality of "intellectual and moral endowments." These he said, *might* be unequal ... "*perhaps.*"

Many causes, including prominently the religious conviction that all men are brothers, conspired to change public opinion in the United States towards the end of the Civil War. The Emancipation Proclamation, by altering the legal status of slaves and by encouraging them to flee their masters and seek refuge in the Union armies, had some effect. But the greatest source of the change was probably the testimony given in blood by the

11 In fact, it was in the Peoria speech. The text there runs, "whether this [feeling against equality] accords with justice and sound judgement, is not the sole question, if indeed, it is any part of it. A universal feeling, whether well or ill-founded, can not be safely disregarded. We can not, then, make them equals."

black soldiers who had served the Union. The number enlisted was reported by the President to Congress in January of 1864 to be over 100,000,[12] and Lincoln and many others thought that without their services, the war could not have been won. To a complaining Northern politician, James C. Conkling, who objected to fighting "to free negroes," Lincoln penned these memorable words:

> ... [when peace comes] it will then have been proved that, among free men, there can be no successful appeal from the ballot to the bullet; and that they who take such appeal are sure to lose their case, and pay the cost. And then, there will be some black men who can remember that, with silent tongue, and clenched teeth, and steady eye, and well poised bayonet, they have helped mankind on to this great consummation; while, I fear, there will be some white ones, unable to forget that, with malignant heart, and deceitful speech, they have strove to hinder it.
> Lincoln, "Letter to James C. Conkling," August 26, 1863

When a man will not fight to preserve his people and his principles, we call him a slave; when a slave does fight, we see in him a man. In antiquity, slaves who risked their lives to save their masters were often manumitted. They had proved their manhood. Lincoln wrote Conkling in the same letter, "If they stake their lives for us, they must be prompted by the strongest motive—even the promise of freedom. And the promise being made, must be kept."

It cannot, alas, be said that the promise was perfectly kept. It would take a century more after the abolition of slavery for a new exercise of Declaration statesmanship to establish political equality without regard to race in this country. But the start was made in the time of Lincoln's stewardship.

Let us be blunt; if Lincoln had taken the full position of equal social and political rights, he would not have been electable to any statewide office in Illinois, neither in 1854, when he sought election from the Illinois leg-

12 By the end of the war, over 200,000 blacks had served in the Union armed forces, and 37,000 had died serving their country.

islature to the U.S. Senate and nearly won, nor in 1858, when he and Douglas had their memorable debates. He would not have become president in 1860, nor would any member of his party who might take up the banner of full social and political equality. He accomplished the good that he could, always insisting on the fundamental principles that, in the fullness of time, would yield yet more perfect results. To achieve both these goods, he had to rekindle a reverence for the Declaration. Let us look briefly at how he did that in the Peoria speech.

THE POWER OF THE WORD

Words, words, words. "Mere words" men say, and yet it is by the power of words that we take common counsel and learn to govern ourselves. We are free because we are made in the image of the all-wise God, and we have a bit of His light in our minds, and by that bit we strive to live according to His laws, the "laws of nature, and of nature's God." Of divine things, St. Paul writes, "But how are men to call upon him in whom they have not believed? And how are they to believe in him of whom they have never heard? And how are they to hear of him without a preacher?"

Lincoln preached in Peoria. He preached the political religion he had declared must be preached years ago in Springfield. Douglas and the doctrine of popular sovereignty were "giving up the OLD faith...." Human equality and popular sovereignty were "as opposite as God and mammon...." Three times he calls the proposition that all men are created equal, the "ancient faith." Of the Nebraska Bill he says, "It hath no relish of salvation in it." He calls the Founders, "our revolutionary fathers," and "the fathers of the republic," stirring memories of Abraham, Isaac, and Jacob. He compares slavery to the fateful disobedience of Adam. He says: "Our republican robe is soiled, and trailed in the dust. Let us re-purify it. Let us turn and wash it white, in the spirit, if not the blood, of the Revolution."

Lincoln was like a great preacher in more than his scriptural language and his vision that America was founded on the Declaration as a kind of covenant or original creed, the "ancient faith." He endeavored to emulate the charity of great preaching, too, as when he admitted that "the Southern people" were "just what we would be in their situation," and when he said that "I surely will not blame them...." He stressed that Thomas Jefferson, the 'father Abraham' of the American covenant was "a Virginian by birth

... a slaveholder...." He opened his speech by announcing that he did not "propose to question the patriotism, or to assail the motives of any man, or class of men...." He added that he wished "to be no less than national in all the positions" he would take. When he had suggested that "... a gradual emancipation might be adopted ..." he immediately added, "but for their tardiness in this I will not undertake to judge our brethren of the south." Thus, to political faith, he added political charity.

The climax of the speech actually occurs about three-fourths in; after that point Lincoln anticipates some of the points he expects Douglas to make in his final hour's response. The paragraph begins with "Our republican robe is soiled...." It ends with these words of salvation and hope, which we quote in full:

> Let us re-adopt the Declaration of Independence, and with it, the practices, and policy, which harmonize with it. Let north and south—let all Americans—let all lovers of liberty everywhere—join in the great and good work. If we do this, we shall not only have saved the Union; but we shall have so saved it, as to make and keep it, forever worthy of the saving. We shall have so saved it, that the succeeding millions of free happy people, the world over, shall rise up, and call us blessed, to the latest generations.

In the Lyceum speech, Lincoln had concluded by urging the statesmen of his day to take the materials supplied by reason and mold them into intelligence, morality, and reverence for the law. At Peoria, he took his own advice, and became such a statesman.

DRED SCOTT: The Supreme Court Betrays the Declaration

> ... Congress is neither "to legislate slavery into any Territory or State nor to exclude it therefrom, but to leave the people thereof perfectly free to form and regulate their domestic institutions in their own way, subject only to the Constitution of the United States."
>
> A difference of opinion has arisen in regard to the point of time when the people of a Territory shall decide this question for themselves.

> This is, happily, a matter of but little practical importance. Besides, it is a judicial question, which legitimately belongs to the Supreme Court of the United States, before whom it is now pending, and will, it is understood, be speedily and finally settled. To their decision, in common with all good citizens, I shall cheerfully submit, whatever this may be....
>
> The whole Territorial question being thus settled upon the principle of popular sovereignty—a principle as ancient as free government itself—everything of a practical nature has been decided.... Most happy will it be for the country when the public mind shall be diverted from this question to others of more pressing and practical importance.
>
> – President James Buchanan, *Inaugural Address*, March 4, 1857

> I know that Mr. Calhoun and all the politicians of his school denied the truth of the Declaration.... But I say ... that three years ago there had never lived a man who had ventured to assail it in the sneaking way of pretending to believe it, and then asserting it did not include the Negro. I believe the first man who ever said it was Chief Justice Taney in the Dred Scott case, and the next to him was our friend Stephen A. Douglas. And now it has become the catchword of the entire [Democratic] party.
>
> – Abraham Lincoln, *Seventh Debate with Douglas*, Alton, Illinois, October 15, 1858

Dred Scott was a black slave, born in Virginia. His owner, an army officer, had taken him into the free state of Illinois and the then territory of Minnesota, also free soil under the Missouri Compromise of 1820. When Scott's owner died, having willed Scott, Scott's wife, whom he had married in the North, and their children to his wife, Scott sued for his freedom in the state court of Missouri, where the family had been taken and the owner had died. The case reached the United States Supreme Court, which decided against Scott on March 6, 1857, just two days after President Buchanan's inauguration.

Chief Justice Taney's opinion was long and convoluted in its reasoning. The key elements for anti-slavery men were these: It declared that Congress had never had the power to prohibit slavery in the territories, and hence that the Ordinance of 1787 and the Missouri Compromise were never valid, and that blacks were not and could not be citizens of the United States. These were intended by the high court's majority to be legally binding precedents.

Buchanan, who had been in private correspondence with at least two members of the Court prior to their handing down the decision, desired this outcome. It meant that no legal power could prevent the introduction of slaves into federally controlled territory, not only before a territorial government had been set up, but also under the territorial government itself. Neither Congress nor its delegated substitute, the territorial legislature, could do anything whatever to block slavery.

Supreme Court decisions do more than settle the case before them (here, they reduced Scott and his family to the status of slaves again) and establish precedents for closely related future cases. They also include the spirit and reasoning by which future decisions may be made on less closely connected matters. These additional elements of the justices' opinions are called, "*obiter dicta*." In Taney's written opinion, the *obiter dicta* included the claim that the founders did not intend to include blacks in the Constitution or in the Declaration of Independence. Assuming that the humanity of the black man was not a constitutional principle, Taney went on to reason that the operative parts of the Constitution would be those governing him as a species of property. Accordingly, he wrote,

> And no word can be found in the Constitution which gives Congress a greater power over slave property, or which entitles property of that kind to less protection than property of any other description. The only power conferred is the power coupled with the duty of guarding and protecting the owner in his rights.
>
> – Chief Justice Roger B. Taney, *Dred Scott v. Sanford*,1857

The Dred Scott decision provoked a storm of controversy in the North. The nationally known editor of the *New York Tribune*, Horace Greeley, wrote that the decision was about as respectable as an opinion reached by "a majority of those congregated in any Washington bar-room." It also caused both Lincoln and Douglas serious political problems, though for opposite reasons, as we shall see. Let's start with Douglas.

Buchanan had said in his inaugural that the territorial question was being settled on the basis of Douglas' principle of "Popular Sovereignty." In 1854, "Popular Sovereignty" as taught by Douglas meant that the people of a territory would be free to keep slavery out by making a law. Congress had chosen not to make such a law by the repeal of the Missouri Compromise in the Nebraska Bill, but the people of Kansas still could, before they applied to become a state. Now the Court had decided that not only Congress, but also the people of the territory, had no such power. How could Douglas now say that popular sovereignty meant anything? And if, as Lincoln was to hammer home in the great debates of 1858, slavery was hard to abolish once even a sizeable minority of the inhabitants held slaves, did *Dred Scott* mean anything other than the total victory of Calhoun and the more extreme pro-slavery men in the South? After the Court's decision, the only part of the governmental structure in the country that could ban slavery was the state government. Lincoln was to show reason to doubt that sole remaining bulwark's chances to stand.

Lincoln's statesmanship faced a problem of its own. After all, the highest court in the land had declared that the central reason for the existence of his party, the use of the national power to block the expansion of slavery in the territories, was unconstitutional. And Lincoln himself had said in the Lyceum speech that American statesmanship required an almost religious "reverence for the constitution and laws." Was *Dred Scott* not, as a precedent, "the constitution and laws?" Had he not said, just a year ago, that "We [Republicans] will submit to its [the Court's] decisions; and if you [Democrats] do also, there will be an end of the matter?"

Rarely has there been a Supreme Court decision as partisan in its effects as *Dred Scott* ... perhaps never.[13] To save his doctrine of "Popular Sovereignty" in a territory in which the majority opposed slavery, Douglas would have to advocate local resistance to passage of local laws to protect legally held property, i.e., slaves. If the territorial legislature or its subordinate agencies simply refused to enact or enforce the laws needed to help the owner

13 *Roe v. Wade* comes to mind as equally controversial, but the division is neither so partisan nor so sectional as was *Dred Scott.*

hold his slaves, they would run off when they pleased. Douglas' espousal of this policy, to which he was forced by the probing questions of Lincoln in the second of the Lincoln-Douglas debates of 1858, was to lose him every Southern state in the Presidential election of 1860.

On the other hand, Lincoln had said while campaigning for Fremont, the Republican candidate in the 1856 election, that there was only one question, the answer to which defined his party: "Shall the government of the United States prohibit slavery in the [territory of] the United States?" Now his party was to be defined by advocating a position solemnly held to be unconstitutional! What was he to do?

For three months he thought, and held his peace. Then, in June of 1857, after Douglas had joined Taney in holding that the Declaration did not include blacks, who were, according to the Senator, "an inferior race," and "incapable of self-government," Lincoln struck.

In a forceful speech given in Springfield on June 26, 1857, Lincoln withdrew his unqualified promise of acquiescence in the dictates of the Court. He granted that Scott and his family must stay in slavery, granted too that any future decisions made in accordance with that decision as a precedent would bind him as to action, but he emphatically denied that it had any moral force that would keep him or anyone else from direct, peaceful, and legal political measures aimed at its overthrow. Legal precedents have great force if they are unanimous, impartial, consistent with our legal expectations and traditions, including the policy of our statesmen, and if they are based on what is true.

The Dred Scott decision, Lincoln held, met none of these standards. He said, "... we think the ... decision is erroneous. We know the court that made it, has often overruled its own decisions, and we shall do what we can to have it overrule this. We offer no *resistance* to it." Quoting President Andrew Jackson, Lincoln implied that the executive and legislative branches could act in ways contrary to the decision of the court, taken as *precedent* and *authority*. Jackson had said that:

> The Congress, the executive and the court must each for itself be guided by its own opinion of the Constitution. Each public officer, who takes an oath to support the Constitution, swears

> that he will support it *as he understands it*, and not as it is understood by others.
> – President Jackson's Veto Message to the Senate Regarding the Bank of the United States; July 10, 1832 [italics added]

Lincoln drops his argument here, but he has raised a difficult and powerful point. Was he saying that when an egregiously wrong decision has been reached by the Court, that the other branches may legislate and act contrary to it as authority and precedent, and must only go along with the Court's understanding when particular cases are decided? Such a teaching would greatly impair the power of the Court to decide fundamental questions, where public opinion is divided or hostile. It would surely be prudent to resort to it only in matters of great import. But was not slavery such a matter? And without such an understanding of Constitutional Law, how could judicial tyranny be effectively resisted?

The rest of the speech, and the part where it soars, is devoted to showing that it is historically false to say that the black man had no part in the Declaration, and to expounding the Declaration as a standard of human action and a beacon for human hopes. We give two excerpts from the speech, which could, with profit, be read in its entirety:

> ... In those days [the period of the founding], our Declaration of Independence was held sacred by all; but now, to aid in making the bondage of the Negro universal and eternal, it is assailed, and sneered at, and construed, and hawked at, and torn, till, if its framers could rise from their graves, they could not at all recognize it.
>
> ... They [the founders] defined with tolerable distinctness, in what respects they did consider all men created equal—equal in "certain inalienable rights, among which are life, liberty, and the pursuit of happiness." This they said, and this they meant. They did not mean to assert the obvious untruth, that all were then enjoying that equality, nor yet, that they were about to confer it immediately upon them. In fact they had no power to confer such a boon. They meant simply to declare the *right*, so

> that the *enforcement* of it might follow as fast as circumstances should permit. They meant to set up a standard maxim for free society, which could be familiar to all, and revered by all; constantly looked to, constantly labored for, and even though never perfectly attained, constantly approximated, and thereby constantly spreading and deepening its influence, and augmenting the happiness and value of life to all people of all colors everywhere. The assertion that "all men are created equal" was of no practical use in effecting our separation from Great Britain; and it was placed in the Declaration, not for that, but for future use. Its authors meant it to be, thank God, it is now proving itself, a stumbling block to those who in after times might seek to turn a free people into the hateful paths of despotism. They knew the proneness of prosperity to breed tyrants, and they meant when such should re-appear in this fair land and commence their vocation they should find left for them at least one hard nut to crack.
>
> I have now briefly expressed my view of the *meaning* and *objects* of that part of the Declaration of Independence which declares that "all men are created equal."
>
> – Abraham Lincoln, *Speech*, Springfield, Illinois, June 26, 1857

Lincoln perhaps went beyond what was in Jefferson's mind in his account of the meaning of the Declaration. We argued in an earlier chapter that there was great immediate use of the idea of human equality towards effecting our separation from Great Britain. But where Jefferson used equality for separation and revolution, Lincoln saw in it a deeper meaning for perpetuation and justice. Equality in Jefferson's thought led to "don't tread on me," since I am your equal, and I have my rights. And Jefferson was not wrong. But in Lincoln's thought, this old, perhaps selfish, perhaps passionate sense of 'my rights,' while retained, has added to it, what *is* right.

Let's say that again in a slightly different way. In this speech, rights are not only the basis of resistance and possibly revolution, but the standard to be aspired to, looked to, approached, approximated, perhaps never perfectly attained. Slavery remains a violation of rights, but now it is also, and more importantly, *not right*. As Lincoln will say in the next to last debate, when confronted by Douglas's presentation of the rights of the people to choose slavery, to have slaves,

> ... he is perfectly logical if there is nothing wrong in the institution; but if you admit that it is wrong, he cannot logically say that any body has a right to do wrong.

You might almost say that the attack of Taney and Douglas upon the Declaration gave Lincoln a golden opportunity to restore the fortunes both of his party and of the country. It moved Lincoln to take the argument about slavery, which had been mired in discussions of laws and technicalities when conducted by the political 'moderates', and intemperate, uncharitable, and divisive when pressed by abolitionists and Southern "fire-eaters," and restored it to fundamental principles that hold the Union together and give it purpose. It also taught us something about the fallibility of the Supreme Court, a lesson some would have us relearn in our day.

We leave our consideration of Lincoln's Declaration statesmanship here, aware that his story and that of the nation's final struggle with slavery was only to be consummated in the fiery trial of civil war. As we have said before, our subject is not American history, but American *principles.* We have argued that this period of Lincoln's statesmanship was guided by a deep reflection on the principles of the Declaration, and brought about a new and deeper understanding of and love for those principles. A sign that this greater understanding was achieved is that every Congressional Act admitting a new state, starting in 1864 with Nevada and continuing through Hawaii in 1959, has contained a provision specifying that the state government would be faithful to the principles contained in the Declaration of Independence.

Perhaps a word of respect for the courage and honor of the men of the South would be in order here. Most of them fought for hearth and home, whatever the reasons of the political men who brought on the war may have been. Estimates vary, but probably no more than one in three came from a slave-owning household. The spirit and valor of the Confederate armies has impressed everyone who has read the record of their lost cause. The capacity and personal dignity of many Southern generals, particularly Robert E. Lee, have been admired by Americans of all regions and parties from the days of their doomed but gallant campaigns to the present. Lee's views on slavery were those of the days of Jefferson. He wrote his wife in 1856,

> In this enlightened age, there are few I believe, but what will acknowledge, that Slavery as an institution, is a moral, political evil in any Country. It is useless to expatiate on its disadvantages. I think it however a greater evil to the White than to the black race, & while my feelings are strongly enlisted on behalf of the latter, my Sympathies are more strong for the former.

Lee's agonizing choice to join the Southern cause, which historian Samuel Eliot Morrison wrote, "[showed] the distress of a noble mind," is best seen in his own words:

> Secession is nothing but revolution.... In 1808 ... and [when] the Hartford Convention assembled, secession was termed treason by Virginia statesmen; what can it be now? Still, a Union that can only be maintained by swords and bayonets, and in which strife and civil war are to take the place of brotherly love and kindness, has no charm for me. If the Union is dissolved, the government disrupted, I shall return to my native state and share the miseries of my people. Save in her defense, I will draw my sword no more.
> – Col. Robert E. Lee, USA, to his son , January, 1861 (quoted in Samuel Eliot Morrison's *Oxford History of the American People*, page 613)

A recent book on Lee and Grant ends with the following paragraph, which is both touching and merits some reflection:

> In the mid-1970's a government clerk was riffling through old files in a Washington bureau and discovered a yellowed piece of paper dated October 2, 1865.
>
> *'I, Robert E. Lee of Lexington, Virginia do solemnly swear, in the presence of Almighty God, that I will henceforth support, protect*

and defend the Constitution of the United States, and the Union of the States thereunder, and that I will, in like manner, abide by and faithfully support all laws and proclamations which have been made during the existing rebellion with reference to the emancipation of slaves, so help me God.'

No one knew how Lee's oath came to be forgotten in an old file drawer, but it was commonly believed that the notarized document had been hidden in 1865 to suppress evidence that former Confederates were willing to restore the United States. More than a hundred years after his death, Robert E. Lee's oath was finally acted upon and his citizenship restored by the United States House of Representatives. The vote was not unanimous." – From *The Generals*, by Nancy Scott Anderson and Dwight Anderson, p. 470

POSTSCRIPT

Perhaps no other period in American history has been so extensively described by historians as the Civil War and the events leading up to it. Any reading the student does in this area will be beneficial; we make no attempt to cover the wealth of materials that exist, except for the following brief remarks.

Harry V. Jaffa's Crisis of the House Divided, *The University of Chicago Press, 1982, is the best, fullest, and most useful book for the purpose of studying Lincoln's statesmanship in the period leading up to the Civil War, and we heartily recommend it to all our readers. We are deeply indebted to Professor Jaffa. All of the book is outstanding; we particularly recommend Chapter XIV, "The Universal Meaning of the Declaration of Independence." Jaffa's latest book,* A New Birth of Freedom, *Rowman and Littlefield, 2000, should be read by anyone wanting to think through the issue of secession, and the nature of the American Union.*

The Third Volume of Paul Rahe's Republics, Ancient and Modern, *The University of North Carolina Press, 1992, has also proved invaluable.*

For Southern efforts to suppress speech about slavery, William Lee Miller's Arguing About Slavery, *which treats in lively and memorable prose the story of John Quincy Adams and the "gag rule" is the definitive work.*

Miller's recent book, Lincoln's Virtues, *Vintage Books, 2003, is also excellent. Miller calls it, "An Ethical biography," since it considers not the policy or the history of Lincoln's actions, but their basis in his thought and character.*

A reader can get a fine introduction to the abolitionist movement from Henry Mayer's All on Fire, William Lloyd Garrison and the Abolition of Slavery, *St. Martin's Press, 1998.*

The best single volume treatment of the Civil War era, political, social, and military, is James M. McPherson's Battle Cry of Freedom, *Oxford University Press, 1988. We strongly recommend the coverage of the events leading up to the war, chapters, 3–8.*

Original sources are irreplaceable in thoughtful study. Again, a full list would be excessively long, but we cannot forbear urging more reading of Lincoln, and of the Lincoln-Douglas debates, *both of which are available in many editions and forms. Every American should read the* Gettysburg Address *and* Lincoln's Second Inaugural. *Supreme Court decisions, too, are easily obtained from libraries and elsewhere.* Dred Scott *is long, but repays the efforts of a serious student.*

A reader whose interest is piqued by the quotation from President Jackson on coordinate responsibility for Constitutional interpretation might wish to consider how that teaching would apply to the segregation and Jim Crow laws, treated in the next part of this book, and how it would play out as applied to Roe v. Wade, *the abortion case.*

CHAPTER 9
THE STATESMANSHIP OF THE CIVIL RIGHTS MOVEMENT

This section will be much shorter than our treatment of the struggle over slavery, and it will culminate in events much closer to our own time. We will look at the failure to realize the equality promised in the Fourteenth and Fifteenth Amendments to the Constitution and see once again the living force of appeals to the Declaration of Independence, and to its religious roots, in American politics. A look at events following the Civil War is necessary to set the stage.

RECONSTRUCTION AND ITS AFTERMATH: The False Spring of Political and Social Equality

After Lincoln's re-election in November of 1864, the President, in his annual message to Congress, recommended the adoption of an amendment to the Constitution abolishing slavery. Congress passed the amendment on January 31st 1865; it was ratified by the states on December 6th of that same year. With the surrender of the Confederate armies in the spring of 1865, the war had come to an end. Lincoln had been pondering how to reconcile the states that had been in rebellion; his famous Second Inaugural, while stating no policy, proposed the spirit in which Americans should act: "With malice toward none; with charity for all; with firmness in the right, as God gives us to see the right, let us strive on to finish the work we are in; to bind up the nation's wounds…." What that would have meant no one can know. Lincoln was taken from this life by the assassin's bullet, dying on the morning of April 15th. His Vice-President, Democrat Andrew Johnson of Tennessee, and the Congress, dominated by the Republican Party, would have to undertake the task of restoring the Union and dealing with the emancipated slaves.

The *Oxford History* states that the economic conditions in the South were worse than those in Central Europe after either of the World Wars. Deaths in both armies had been at levels similar to those experienced by the European powers—much higher, in proportion to the population, than those America suffered in the Second World War. Nonetheless, there was remarkably little bitterness or resistance to the verdict of the battlefield. Lee and the other Southern chieftains counseled acquiescence and reunion, and civilian governments were quickly set up in all the states of the former Confederacy. Since there was some doubt about the current relation of the rebellious states to the Union, and since the state governments were in need of some reconstitution—at the very least, their ordinances of secession would have to be repealed—a period of reconstruction was called for.

What would happen, what *should* happen, to the former slaves, the "freedmen," as they were called? Sentiment in the North was still not altogether friendly to full "social and political equality," as Lincoln had termed it. Few blacks voted or served on juries in the North, and racial bigotry was strong there. Those who had looked ahead to the day when slavery was no more were not necessarily thinking of an integrated society. Many, including Lincoln, had talked, and sometimes acted, to colonize free blacks in Africa or in some other distant and largely open land.

Whether such a scheme was just or practicable is not especially relevant; no one moved to muster the political and financial power needed to effect it, and surely the freedmen themselves had little desire for resettlement. Those freedmen, and their black brethren who had served in the Union armies, had the manliness and independence of mind that military veterans often have, and were not about to be treated as servile or inferior creatures. But the federal executive power, now wielded by a Democrat, Andrew Johnson, would not be deployed forcefully to attain a complete social and political equality regime on the overwhelmingly Democratic Southern State governments and their majority white citizens. "Presidential Reconstruction" as it has been called, with Johnson as President, would be tepid, not fierce.

Moreover, the war had been fought by the Lincoln Administration on the legal premise that the Southern states were in the Union, and only violently and temporarily controlled by rebels. Accordingly, as soon as state governments loyal to the Union were reconstituted, they were acknowledged by President Johnson, even if dominated by anti-freedmen sentiments. Many weighty political actions dealing with the new order following the abolition of slavery would be up to these reconstituted state governments themselves.

Without giving excessive detail, let it be said, in brief, that these governments did too little good, and too much that was positively harmful. Perhaps they need not have granted full citizenship to all freedmen, without a probationary period of education and economic help, as even some abolitionists had recommended. But they should not have enacted the "black codes," which limited freedom of contract, travel, and employment, and which were felt to amount almost to a re-imposition of slavery. Perhaps they should have enacted universal suffrage (voting rights), but failing in that, they should have allowed at least returning black soldiers and the well educated freedmen to vote. They most certainly should not have tolerated mobs' burning schools set up by the federally run Freedmen's Bureau (established in 1865 and run by the War Department) to help the black man rise to the dignity and duties of citizenship.

The good they did do, including such fundamental things as recognizing the legitimacy of black marriages and their rights to sue and be sued, was not enough to overcome the indignation kindled by the black codes and other burdens they placed on the freedmen. It seemed to many, black and white, who had fought and sacrificed for the Union cause that the victory won in the war was slipping away, and that the old order of slavery, or rather, a *de facto* equivalent, was on the rise. A reaction was soon to come from the North.

Historians call the second phase of Reconstruction, "Radical Reconstruction." It began in the spring and summer of 1866, with the passage, over the President's veto, of the first federal Civil Rights Act of 1866 and the Fourteenth Amendment, which would be ratified in 1868; both laws, if enforced, would overturn the black codes and establish equal citizenship for all freedmen and their descendants. In 1869–70 Congress authorized and President Grant set up a Federal Department of Justice to see to the enforcement of the Civil Rights Act and other federal law. Before then, there had been no such department, no regular police duties for federal marshals, and no significant role for the Attorney General, who had been merely the President's political lawyer.[14]

The Freedmen's Bureau was reauthorized, with increased powers, bitterly resented in the South. Binding up the nations' wounds now gave way to a second, political civil war. Passions were high in both sections. These issues dominated the mid-term election of 1866, which gave the Republican Party, now bereft of its prudent head, Lincoln, a huge and veto-proof majority in the Congress. President Johnson now became irrelevant, and Congress took the initiative.

The new Congress acted swiftly. Civilian state governments were swept aside, replaced by military governors in five districts covering what had been ten states. These states then adopted new constitutions and laws enfranchising the blacks and disqualifying former Confederate officers; in five states this meant black majorities in registered voters. To the Republican politicians who engineered it, it presumably meant Republican electoral power all across the South. These states were not allowed congressional representation until they had ratified the Fourteenth Amendment, which understandably enjoyed less than potent authority in the South when white politicians recovered their power a decade later. To ensure that the local governments would respect the civil rights of the Fourteenth Amendment, another amendment was added, the Fifteenth, prohibiting the denial or abridgment of the right of citizens of the United States to vote by "the

14 By 1870, after the end of the Civil War, the increase in the amount of litigation involving the United States had required the very expensive retention of a large number of private attorneys to handle the workload. A concerned Congress passed the Act to Establish the Department of Justice (ch. 150, 16 Stat. 162), creating "an executive department of the government of the United States" with the Attorney General as its head. The following is from the Department of Justice:

> Officially coming into existence on July 1, 1870, the Department of Justice was empowered to handle all criminal prosecutions and civil suits in which the United States had an interest. To assist the Attorney General, the 1870 Act also created the Office of the Solicitor General, who represents the interests of the United States before the U.S. Supreme Court.

The 1870 Act remains the foundation for the Department's authority.

United States or by any state on account of race, color, or previous condition of servitude." This was meant to insure the black voters in the South against local intimidation, but its universal language would reasonably apply to naturalized or native-born American citizens of Mexican or Chinese ancestry wishing to vote in California, for example.

Despite these strong measures on behalf of the newly liberated blacks, Southern state governments in the next few years were never in fact dominated by freedmen; there was only one black governor, P.B.S. Pinchback of Louisiana, and he served exactly 35 days, from Dec. 9, 1872 to January 13, 1873. There was never a majority of freedmen in both houses of any state legislature, and only one black man on any state supreme court. Contrary to the bitter complaints of many ex-confederates, the south was never ruled by blacks, and was never likely to be so ruled.

Instead, a three-part coalition formed in the reconstructing states. It was composed of Republican newcomers from the North, derisively termed "carpetbaggers," Southerners who thought it best to cooperate with the new regimes like Lee's right hand man, General James T. Longstreet, and the freedmen themselves. The politicians of this coalition, overwhelmingly the white politicians, held the reins of power for only a few years—no more than ten in any state—and though there were men, white and black, of talent and integrity among them, the performance of these governments was mixed. Voting rights and civil rights were equalized throughout the region, a striking fact when contrasted with the North, where blacks had voted in only a few states. Public education was greatly extended; the public school systems of the South generally date from the years of radical reconstruction. Public works and what we would now call "social services" were initiated or extended. Largely in consequence of these new governmental functions, taxes and public debts skyrocketed. Moreover corruption was open and extensive, though it must be added, political corruption is always with us, and was equally gross in parts of the North, especially in the urban centers like New York City.

The mood of the white and formerly pro-confederate majority, who felt, and sometimes were, left out of these political arrangements, turned ugly, their actions often violent. Lynchings and intimidation were the order of the day; the period saw the birth of the Ku Klux Klan and other vigilante groups. One of the purposes of this intimidation (terrorism, really) was reduction of the black vote. Another was the destruction of the most talented or assertive of the Republican political leadership, especially the black Republicans. Vandalism, beatings, and even murder were employed against officeholders, and at one point, Sept. 14, 1874, an armed mob attacked the statehouse in New Orleans to overturn contested Republican electoral victories in Louisiana. Gen. Longstreet led a force of police and black state militia against the insurrectionists, but he was defeated and there were serious casualties—over one hundred dead and wounded on both sides. President Grant had to send five thousand United States Army regulars and three gunboats to restore order and to reinstate the legally elected representatives. In December, the President sent for his toughest and most trusted commander, Gen. Phil Sheridan. Sheridan arrived at the end of the year, and found the Democrats using force to seat five of their party members in the Louisiana House. Sheridan's soldiers ejected the five Democrats on January 4th, and the remaining Democrats walked out in protest. Grant backed up "Little Phil," and the White League beat a retreat in New Orleans for a time. Press reaction in the North was critical of the administration, but a Congressional investigation found Grant's and Sheridan's actions proper.

Although the federal government made efforts to suppress the Klan and to put down the worst of the violent and illegal political actions, these crimes continued to resurface. Under the pressure of the white resistance, and weakened by the corruption the radical reconstruction governments had spawned, or at the least, tolerated, the coalition shrank and fractured, while its Northern patron, the Republican Party, alarmed at the reports of corruption and debt, and still undermined by anti-black prejudice, grew weary of protecting it. It may seem hard to understand a century and a quarter later, but Grant's firm and just action in Louisiana in 1874 and 1875 actually hurt him and his party.

Weakness in the national political will to support the Radical Republicans' power in the formerly Confederate states, and the increasing strength of the white resistance there, led to an end of this phase of reconstruction by 1877. In the next 20 years, the Republican Party virtually ceased to exist in the former confederate states, but the newly empowered Democrat governments, the so-called "Redeemers," moderated and controlled the worst of the race-hatred from the days of reconstruction. The situation was unstable and uneven, a mixture of paternalism, considerable social mixing of the races, subtle and not so subtle oppression, and much black self-help and progress. But it was emphatically the White Man's rule, and marked the end of the most hopeful era for equality in the South for almost a century. This story has been told with great conviction and much exaggeration by all sides; our purpose has been not so much to settle old controversies as to understand the background for the next Declaration struggle, the defiance of the Fourteenth and Fifteenth Amendments and the victory of equal rights in the 1960's.

MOB RULE, POPULISM, AND JIM CROW

It is a common misconception, indicative of prejudice against the South, that systematic oppression of the black man in the form of legally enforced segregation commenced immediately after the withdrawal of the protective umbrella of the federal power in the 1870's. This is substantially false. For two more decades, many blacks continued to exercise their constitutional right to vote, and much of the public transportation system was not racially segregated, to name only two facts contradicting this view. Moreover, state governments included elected and appointed black officers, and there was black representation from the Southern states in Congress up to 1901. In Louisiana, where the cosmopolitan influence of the great city of New Orleans was strong, there were 130,334 "colored people" registered to vote in 1896, according to the *Oxford History*. Eight years later, however, the number was 1,342. Similar drops occurred all over the South in the 1890's.

What happened? The story is convoluted and ironic. At first, the lawless and resentful faction in the South, which had continued the abominable practices of lynching and terror on and off through this period, turned against the Redeemer state governments, the "conservatives," many of them former officers in the Confederate armies, like Governor Wade Hampton of South Carolina. This was largely a reaction from below, a populist movement of the small farmer and working man, envious of the wealth and privilege enjoyed by the men of business who ran the government and bought their crops and labor at low prices and sold them for what seemed to these working men unjust profits. At first, the populists welcomed support from the freedmen, who, of course, shared economic grievances with the poor white farmers. When the conservatives used their power to steal black votes and intimidate black voters to help stem the rising populist tide, the populists then turned on the blacks, and, strangely and tragically, formed, together with the conservatives, a coalition grounded on hostility to social and political equality for blacks. Segregation and disenfranchisement were now the explicit goals of the new white majority. These objectives became central to the Democratic party's political order in the South for the next 60 years.

Similar racist sentiments and economic fears in the West led to the formation of a virulently anti-Chinese 'Workingman's Party" which was involved in vigilantism and riots in San Francisco and elsewhere in California. Nor were these excesses confined to the recovering South and the unruly West.

In 1908, within a half mile of Lincoln's Springfield, Illinois home, there was a vile case of lynching of two blacks by a white mob. The violence was set off by a white woman's accusation of a black man, George Richardson, of rape. She subsequently testified to a grand jury that Richardson had nothing to do with the rape, and the authorities tried to remove him and another black man to a safe location. A mob, furious at their departure, went wild, destroying property and killing two other blacks with no connection to the case. The governor had to call out the militia, to the number of five thousand men, to restore order. This was the very lawlessness proceeding from democracy and the passions that Lincoln had warned against in the Lyceum speech.

In short, it was a time of populism everywhere in the country; and in places like California, the lower Midwest, and the South, where populism easily blended with racism, the results were ugly. The astonishing drop in voter registration in Louisiana is a sign of the re-imposition of race-conscious law in many parts of the country but especially and systematically in the South. During these years, white labor found, or thought it found, a protection against black competition in laws that restricted blacks or segregated them in the workplace, requiring employers to construct separate entrances or separate toilet facilities, for example. Public schools and transportation were segregated, and black participation in the basic civic duties, not only voting, but also jury duty and public employment, were also sharply reduced, all by the power of state laws. The legislative acts that produced this effect were termed the "Jim Crow" laws, named after a colloquial Southern expression for the black man.

Jim Crow was a shameless attempt, at the state level, to nullify the 14th

and 15th Amendments. And these amendments sprang from Declaration principles! Why was this scofflaw attitude not resisted by the nation as a whole? A partial answer may be found in the intellectual and academic currents moving through the nation from the 1870's well into the 20th Century. Pseudo-scientific racism, drawing its origins from Darwin's work, or as it is sometimes called, "Social Darwinism," and Germanic Historicism, springing from Hegel, undermined the Declaration principles of human equality and the eternal natural law and natural rights. Perhaps the most influential American Historian in the first part of the 20th century was Charles Beard. In 1908, Beard said this of the intellectual movements in the period we are reviewing:

> ... in comparing the political writings of the last twenty-five years with earlier treatises one is struck with decreasing reference to the doctrine of natural rights as a basis for political practice. The theory has been rejected ... because we have come to recognize since Darwin's day that the nature of things, once supposed to be eternal, is itself a stream of tendency.

and, in the same lecture, Beard said:

> Locke mistakenly depended upon an understanding of nature, using abstract reason, rather than history, and the method of science, to understand politics.... The influence of the historical school on correct thinking in politics has been splendidly supplemented by that of the Darwinians.
> – From *Politics*, a lecture delivered at Columbia University, 1908

Beard was active in the Progressive movement, whose most famous academic politician, Woodrow Wilson, became President in 1912. Wilson's stance on Declaration Principles is summarized in a recent essay by Professor Ronald J. Pestritto, Dean of the Graduate School at Hillsdale College. Pestritto writes:

> Perhaps the greatest obstacle to a progressive constitutionalism, according to Wilson, was that the founders' constitutional order

> rested upon the notion that the ends of government are permanent: namely, the protection of individual rights that are derived from the transhistorical 'laws of nature and of nature's God'.... As long as the preeminence of individual natural rights was maintained, Wilson knew that it would be difficult to change the institutional arrangements of the Constitution, which were designed primarily to protect individuals from majority faction.
> – *Challenges to the American Founding*, ed. Pestritto and West, ch. 10

In those times, Social Darwinism, the rise of the social sciences and the decline of traditional philosophy, naked human *amour proper*, and the imperialism of the Spanish American War all contributed to a "respectable" racism. C. Vann Woodward writes in *The Strange Career of Jim Crow*: "At home and abroad, biologists, sociologists, anthropologists, and historians, as well as journalists and novelists, gave support to the doctrine that races were discrete entities and that the 'Anglo-Saxon' or 'Caucasian' was the superior of them all."

An example of the novelists Woodward had in mind was surely Thomas Dixon, author of *The Clansman*, the novel that was turned into the classic, and utterly white supremacist film, *Birth of a Nation*. The film had a screening in the East Room of the White House, with President Wilson, a college classmate of Dixon's, in attendance. There is a story that Wilson called the film, "true," though in response to protest from the Boston chapter of the NAACP, Wilson's press Secretary denied the story. However that may be, we know that Wilson supported the new race-conscious measures we have been covering in this chapter. With President Wilson in office, the District of Columbia, which was under Congressional rule, became as segregated by law as was Georgia. Starting in 1913, a number of federal agencies were officially segregated, including the Post Office Department and the Bureau of the Census. Workers who complained were fired. President Wilson himself wrote the editor of a religious journal, the *Congregationalist*, in September of 1913, defending his actions: "I would say that I do approve of the segregation that is being attempted in several of the departments."[15]

15 Wilson to Rev. H.A. Bridgman, Sept. 8, 1913, cited in *Woodrow Wilson and the Progressive Era*, by Arthur S. Link.

A large faction of the Democratic Party was active in its resistance to realizing the promises of the Fourteenth and Fifteenth Amendments. What about the role of the Republican Party a generation after Lincoln? A newspaper from the Republican (and old abolitionist) stronghold of Massachusetts contained this brief description of the new state of affairs:

> [Southern race policy was] now the policy of the Administration of the very party which carried the country into and through a civil war to free the slave.[16]

The reference was to the Republican Administration of William McKinley.

Consider the following. Thirty years after the union victory in the Civil War, McKinley staked his political fortune on the claim that the union's preservation was complete. It may be granted that it is a human failing to become entrenched in old battles long after the event and it is no doubt often the part of wisdom to point out that it is time to move on, to draw the curtain of forgetfulness over disputes heavy with years and murky in their causes. This is particularly the case when the artificial perpetuation of such disputes prevents fruitful and edifying new friendships and common endeavor. We can almost hear McKinley inviting his fellow Americans, Northern and Southern, to join him in the common effort of building a bridge to the 20th century, and burying the animosities and divisions of the distant past. Thus, in his 1897 inaugural, he says "The North and the South no longer divide on the old lines.... It will be my constant aim to do nothing, and permit nothing to be done, that will arrest or disturb this growing sentiment of unity and cooperation...."

It sounds impressive. But it does raise a question ... what exactly were the issues and divisions that were being left behind? Were they the kind that the national soul was wise to turn away from? What might it have been that McKinley suspected would require his "constant" attention, lest it "arrest or disturb this growing sentiment of unity and cooperation"?

In 1890, as head of the Ways and Means Committee in Congress, McKinley pushed through a major tariff bill. Some Senators blocked this bill and the Sherman Silver Purchase Act, demanding as their price that the

16 Boston Evening *Transcript*, Jan.14th, 1899, cited in Woodward, p. 73.

GOP give up on a voting rights bill to protect the deteriorating access of Southern blacks to the ballot box. This voting rights bill, to which McKinley gave lip service, was called for by the Republican platform, urged by President Harrison, and passed in the House by a *partisan* 155–149 vote. The choice was between the human rights of black men, and silver and the tariff. The GOP leadership, including, prominently, McKinley, chose Mammon.

The repression of blacks, including Jim Crow laws and lynchings, intensified. The tariff bill is often cited as one of the chief instances of McKinley's "superb" political skills. 1892 saw the apex of lynchings—226 dead that year, 155 of them blacks. Lynching totals for 1889–1918 are 2522 blacks and 702 others. Between 1889 and 1893, the GOP was back in power, and made some efforts to enforce voting rights in accordance with the 15th Amendment.

In 1896, the year of McKinley's first election, the Supreme Court handed down its decision in Plessy v. Ferguson, establishing the famous "separate but equal" doctrine for meeting the due process and equal protection clauses of the 14th Amendment. The decision, in effect, constitutionally authorized Jim Crow laws, which proliferated as a result.

The McKinley administration directed its attention from the beginning to economic and foreign affairs, as the deterioration of the condition of American blacks intensified. In 1901, George White, of North Carolina, the last elected black congressman from the old Confederacy, left the House. There would be no more until 1965. McKinley in his second inaugural address stated that, "sectionalism has disappeared. Division on public questions can no longer be traced by the war maps of 1861. These old differences less and less disturb the judgment."

In 1899, a group of "Massachusetts Negroes" wrote an eloquent, principled, and heart-breaking open letter to President McKinley, (you can find it in a wonderful old collection of original documents in American history and statesmanship, called, *Annals of America).*
which read in part as follows:

> We, colored people of Massachusetts in mass meeting assembled to consider our oppressions and the state of the country relative to the same, have resolved to address ourselves to you in an open letter, notwithstanding your extraordinary, your

incomprehensible silence on the subject of our wrongs in your annual and other messages to Congress, as in your public utterances to the country at large. We address ourselves to you, sir, not as suppliants, but as of right, as American citizens, whose servant you are, and to whom you are bound to listen, and for whom you are equally bound to speak, and upon occasion to act, as for any other body of your fellow countrymen in like circumstances.

We ask nothing for ourselves at your hands, as Chief Magistrate of the republic, to which all American citizens are not entitled. We ask for the enjoyment of life, liberty, and the pursuit of happiness equally with other men. We ask for the free and full exercise of all the rights of American freemen guaranteed to us by the Constitution and laws of the Union, which you were solemnly sworn to obey and execute. We ask you for what belongs to us by the high sanction of Constitution and law, and the democratic genius of our institutions and civilization.

These rights are everywhere throughout the South denied to us, violently wrested from us by mobs, by lawless legislatures, and nullifying conventions, combinations, and conspiracies, openly, defiantly, under your eyes, in your constructive and actual presence. And we demand, which is a part of our rights, protection, security in our life, our liberty, and in the pursuit of our individual and social happiness under a government, which we are bound to defend in war, and which is equally bound to furnish us in peace protection, at home and abroad.

We have suffered, sir God knows how much we have suffered! since your accession to office, at the hands of a country professing to be Christian, but which is not Christian; from the hate and violence of a people claiming to be civilized, but who are not civilized; and you have seen our sufferings, witnessed from your high place our awful wrongs and miseries, and yet you have at no time and on no occasion opened your lips on our behalf.

The Annals of America, vol. 12, ed. by Mortimer J. Adler, Encyclopedia Britannica

Note the explicitly Declarationist language employed in this appeal: "We ask for the enjoyment of life, liberty, and the pursuit of happiness equally with other men." One wonders why it had no effect on McKinley, who had served in the Union armies 35 years earlier, and had his nickname, "the Major" from that service.

A substantial residue of the old civil rights heritage did continue in the GOP through this period. There is a moving and eloquent letter[17] on the subject of equality of rights from President Calvin Coolidge. This is an excerpt:

> The suggestion of denying any measure of their full political rights to such a great group of our population as the colored people is one which, however it might be received in some other quarters, could not possibly be permitted by one who feels a responsibility for living up to the traditions and maintaining the principles of the Republican Party.

The more than fifty years from the triumph of Jim Crow to the successful modern Civil Rights movement offer a rich field for historical inquiry, but the details are too manifold for coverage in this book. We mentioned above the little-known fact that Southern Democrat Woodrow Wilson oversaw, and approved, the *de jure* segregation of much of the federal government. Another Southern Democrat, Harry S. Truman, made a dramatic move in the opposite direction, opening all the Armed Services of the United States to men of all races in 1948–9. Truman himself was moved by the sacrifice of black soldiers in the Second World War, and indignant at the treatment some of those men had received upon returning to their native land. Something of the same sentiment had moved the leaders of the Republican Party in the postbellum period. One wonders why there was not a similar sentiment after the First World War. Could it have been the pseudo-scientific racial theories of the time?[18]

17 Letter from President Coolidge to a Mr. Charles F. Gardner, Fort Hamilton N.Y., August 9, 1924, in *Foundations of the Republic, speeches and addresses,* by Calvin Coolidge, Charles Scribner's Sons, New York and London, 1926. On the internet at https://www.coolidgefoundation.org/resources/speeches-as-president-1923-1928-8/.

18 The subject is discussed in, among other places, John Hope Franklin's *From Slavery to Freedom,* chapters 24–5.

In this account we have paid little attention to the actions of the freedmen themselves. We were looking instead at the application, and in this case, the tragic absence, of Declaration Statesmanship on the part of the leaders of the day, and these were nearly all whites. But, it cannot be said often enough, political self-government requires personal self-government, and there is a long and impressive story of success in the lives of the freedmen and their families which we will only notice. Justice is done to that story by other authors, notably Alan Keyes in his book, *Masters of the Dream.* Suffice it to say here that under the persecution of the Klan, unequal application of the law, widespread strict segregation in nearly all aspects of public social life after 1900, and with the weight of prejudice, and sometimes hatred weighing them down, the free blacks of the South nevertheless advanced in education and financial independence, lived a vibrant church and community life, and sustained and strengthened their families. This last point may surprise contemporary readers who are aware of and lament the breakdown of the American family, and especially the plague of family problems that beset blacks today. But it is a fact. The vast majority of black children born under Jim Crow grew up in marriage-based, two-parent households, in spite of poverty and prejudice.[19]

THE DECLARATION POLITICS OF THE CIVIL RIGHTS MOVEMENT

A Proclamation

> ... Dr. King's activism was rooted in the true patriotism that cherishes America's ideals and strives to narrow the gap between those ideals and reality. He took his stand, he once explained, "because of my love for America and the sublime principles of liberty and equality on which she is founded." He wanted "to transform the jangling discords of our Nation into a beautiful symphony of brotherhood."

19 For this section and the next, we recommend Alan L. Keyes', *Masters of the Dream: The Strength and Betrayal of Black America.* Also, C. Vann Woodward's *The Strange Career of Jim Crow,* Eric Foner's *Reconstruction: America's Unfinished Revolution,* and Jean Edward Smith's fine biography, *Grant.* There are many more books on the progress and setbacks of the rights of American blacks; these four are outstanding.

The majesty of his message, the dignity of his bearing, and the righteousness of his cause are a lasting legacy. In a few short years he changed America for all time. He made it possible for our Nation to move closer to the ideals set forth in our Declaration of Independence: that all people are created equal and are endowed with inalienable rights that government has the duty to respect and protect.

Twenty-three years ago, Dr. King spoke to a quarter of a million Americans gathered near the Lincoln Memorial in Washington—and to tens of millions more watching on television. There he held up his dream for America like a bright banner:

"I have a dream," he said, "that my four little children will one day live in a Nation where they will not be judged by the color of their skin, but by the content of their character.... This will be the day when all of God's children will be able to sing with new meaning, `My country 'tis of thee, sweet land of liberty, of thee I sing.'"

Let all Americans continue to carry forward the banner that 18 years ago fell from Dr. King's hands.... Today we honor him with speeches and monuments. But let us do more. Let all Americans of every race and creed and color work together to build in this blessed land a shining city of brotherhood, justice, and harmony. This is the monument Dr. King would have wanted most of all.

By Public Law 98–144, the third Monday in January of each year has been designated as a public holiday in honor of the "Birthday of Martin Luther King, Jr."

Now, Therefore, I, Ronald Reagan, President of the United States of America, do hereby proclaim Monday, January 20, 1986, as Martin Luther King, Jr. Day.

In Witness Whereof, I have hereunto set my hand this eighteenth day of January, in the year of our Lord nineteen hundred and eighty-six, and of the Independence of the United States of America the two hundred and tenth.

– Ronald Reagan, January 18, 1986

> Our Constitution is color-blind, and neither knows nor tolerates classes among citizens.... It is to be regretted that this high tribunal, the final expositor of the fundamental law of the land, has reached the conclusion that it is competent for a state to regulate the enjoyment by citizens of their civil rights solely upon the basis of race. In my opinion, the judgment this day rendered will, in time, prove to be quite as pernicious as the decision made by this tribunal in the Dred Scott Case.
> – Justice John Marshall Harlan, dissent, *Plessy v. Ferguson*, 1896

Jim Crow reigned unchecked for nearly six decades, until the passage of the 1964 Civil Rights Act and the 1965 Voting Rights Act. Justice delayed for six decades (or even a century, if one goes back to the end of the Civil War) must be regarded as a national failure. Part of the reason for this failure was the United States Supreme Court's unwillingness to defend the Fourteenth and Fifteenth Amendments. But a deeper failure took place in the citizenry. We all failed, North, South, East, and West, to live up to our principles.

But our principles are powerful things, and though they may sleep in the hearts of Americans, they have never yet died. The second half of the 20th century saw a revival of Declaration thought in the legal arena, the religious and moral life, and the political world. Jim Crow was beaten by preaching, teaching, and lawsuits. Perhaps we should not say the victory was final or total, especially in the legal and political world, where Declaration principles are still striving to be realized in the fight against preferential treatment based on race and sex. Still, this part of our story is chiefly a tale of victory, a victory won largely on the basis of explicit and powerful use of the Declaration in our common life as Americans. It, too, is a case of Declaration Statesmanship.

THE COURTS: From Separate but Equal to Equal?

The words of Justice Harlan quoted above come from his prophetic dissent in a Louisiana case in which the majority of the court upheld the right of that state to require a railway company to separate the races in its passenger coaches. Since the law takes rail service to be a public matter, and properly regulated by the state, the issue came down to whether the laws of a state could make a racial distinction between American citizens. That the black passengers who were to be segregated were American citizens was due to the Fourteenth Amendment, which overturned the part of the Dred Scott decision that held that blacks could not be U.S. citizens. Ever since the ratification of the Fourteenth Amendment, all persons born in the United States are, as the Amendment says, "citizens of the United States and of the state wherein they reside." The Constitution is color-blind with regard to citizenship.

Color-blind citizenship is strongly suggested by Declaration principles, but for particular reasons it might not always be obligatory. Citizenship is a right in a political community, and governed by positive human law. Aliens do not become citizens by residence only; they must even now be "naturalized." The liberty that the founders declared to be an inalienable right is principally the freedom to live one's own life, tend to one's own business, travel freely, and, as Lincoln said to Douglas, "to eat the bread, without the leave of anybody else, which his own hand earns." A nation could live by Declaration principles, respecting liberty, and yet embracing a number, perhaps a large number, of free persons who are essentially resident aliens, like the guest workers in Germany and elsewhere. These free persons, who are not members of the civic community, have rights that must be respected, but they need not, and unless they become citizens, must not, vote, serve on juries, and the like. But they miss an important part of their full human potential if they are not eligible for the duties and advantages of citizenship. That was implied by Aristotle long ago, when he said that man was by nature a political animal.

You ought to have a good reason to deny citizenship to any group of inhabitants of your country, especially those who themselves were born there, or even whose parents and grandparents were born there. Your country will be their "native land," and they will be its "native sons." Though the founders, and almost all white Americans, once doubted whether black and white could ever be friends and brothers enough to justify universal black citizenship, the decision was made when the Fourteenth and Fifteenth Amendments were passed. There were even stronger doubts about whether Asians and whites could be in a single political community. Chinese culture seemed more removed from the American way than did the life of the freedmen, and restrictions on Eastern immigration reflected these doubts throughout the late 19th and early 20th century. Indeed, at the time of our Revolution, many Americans were concerned that the French would not make good citizens!

We have said above that black soldiers' valor in the Civil War was partly responsible for the change of heart. So, doubtless, were the bonds of religion and a common language. Fear that the freedmen could not defend themselves without citizens' rights was also a factor, as was Republican electoral self-interest.

Once you have decided to include anyone as a citizen, he immediately has civil rights. The chief of these is equal treatment under the law. But since there was a track record of unequal treatment right after the Civil War, the Fourteenth Amendment went on to insist that the states must guarantee to all citizens equal treatment, regardless of race, and that the federal government would have the power to ensure that they would get it.

Harlan's reasoning in the railway segregation case was clear and simple; citizenship was color-blind, civil rights were equal without regard to color, public access to public railways was part of civil freedom, therefore it was unconstitutional for Louisiana to, as he said, "... [separate] citizens, on the basis of race, while they are on a public highway."

Here is the conclusion of his dissent. As you read it, you may want to recall that his home state was Kentucky, and that he had been, before the War, a slaveholder:

> I am of opinion that the statute of Louisiana is inconsistent with the personal liberty of citizens, white and black, in that state, and hostile to both the spirit and letter of the Constitution of the United States. If laws of like character should be enacted in the several states of the Union, the effect would be in the highest degree mischievous. Slavery, as an institution tolerated by law, would, it is true, have disappeared from our country; but there would remain a power in the states, by sinister legislation, to interfere with the full enjoyment of the blessings of freedom, to regulate civil rights, common to all citizens, upon the basis of race, and to place in a condition of legal inferiority a large body of American citizens, now constituting a part of the political community, called the "People of the United States," for whom,

> and by whom through representatives, our government is administered. Such a system is inconsistent with the guaranty given by the constitution to each state of a republican form of government, and may be stricken down by congressional action, or by the courts in the discharge of their solemn duty to maintain the supreme law of the land, anything in the constitution or laws of any state to the contrary notwithstanding.
>
> For the reason stated, I am constrained to withhold my assent from the opinion and judgement of the majority.
>
> –Justice Harlan, Dissent to *Plessy v. Ferguson, 1896 Supreme Court Reporter*, vol. 16, p. 1148

Perhaps the most famous act of the United States Supreme Court between the notorious cases of *Dred Scott* and *Roe v. Wade* is the 1954 *Brown v. Board of Education* Decision. By its ruling, the Court made racially segregated public schools illegal. Most Americans will tell you that this decision meant that the Court had finally read the letter of the Fourteenth Amendment in the spirit of the Declaration; all men are created equal, and the Constitution is color-blind. Lawyers for the National Association for the Advancement of Colored People (NAACP) had made just such a point in arguing to the Court that school segregation ought to be struck down. Their briefs included passages like these: "... the Fourteenth Amendment prevents states from according differential treatment to American children on the basis of their color or race.... The broad general purpose of the Fourteenth Amendment [is the] obliteration of race and color distinctions ... that the Constitution is color-blind is our dedicated belief." And they won their case. The Court did strike down the segregated schools of Topeka, Kansas.

But arguments before the Court are not the law; the Court gives its own reasons for its decisions, and these are the binding interpretations for other judges, and the precedents for future Supreme Court decisions. Unhappily, most Americans have the wrong idea about *Brown v. Board of Education.* The Court did indeed outlaw segregation, but not because it accepted Harlan's 1896 dissent, that the "Constitution is color-blind." Instead, it ruled that the psychological harm it believed segregation inflicted on black school children was an unlawful injury. This may be true; it may be provable, psychologically, that segregation produces unjust "feelings of inferiority" in the minority child. But even if it is, by deciding the case on this basis, the Court missed the chance to re-establish the fundamental principle of equal justice without regard to color in the law.

This failure would show up in the question of race-conscious policy adopted to ensure equality of results by group twenty years later, when the Court began to consider the legality of "affirmative action." The most famous of these cases was to be *Regents of the University of California v. Bakke,* (1978), in which Justice Brennan was to put the following in his opinion:

> The position ... summed up by the shorthand phrase 'our Constitution is color-blind' ... has never been adopted by this court as the proper meaning of the Equal Protection Clause [of the Fourteenth Amendment]. Indeed, we have expressly rejected this proposition on a number of occasions.

More recent Court rulings have moved, slowly, towards Harlan's color-blind doctrine, but it has yet to be adopted. At present, the government may treat Americans differently on the basis of race, but it must have strong reasons to do so. In the words of Justice O'Connor in *Adarand v. Pena* (1995), "All racial classifications, imposed by whatever federal, state, or local governmental actor, must be analyzed by a reviewing court under strict scrutiny." Strict scrutiny is hard to survive, but not impossible. As of this writing, there are hundreds of federal and state programs and judicial dictates that still treat Americans differently on the basis of race.

From Reconstruction to the present day, then, the courts have not concluded that the principle of equality found in the Declaration and the Fourteenth Amendment, and the promise of a republican form of government consistent with the principles of the Declaration of Independence, require that American law be color-blind. Perhaps it will do so in our lifetimes, but that remains to be seen.

Maybe we expect too much from our courts. The Constitutional structure makes them the most cautious and least creative branch of government, and rightly so. And all of government, even the two more political branches, is finally only the servant of a free and sovereign people. To assess the real progress America has made towards color-blind law, we should turn to our political life, and the hearts and minds of our fellow citizens.

THE SOVEREIGN PEOPLE DECIDES: Scripture and the Declaration as the Roots of the Civil Rights Movement

There is no way one can separate faith from politics in the change of heart that led to the end of Jim Crow and the resolve to live according to the letter and spirit of the Fourteenth and Fifteenth Amendments, culminating in the Civil Rights and Voting Rights legislation of 1964–5. A look at the words of Martin Luther King Jr., who was prominent in securing the passage of both acts, will confirm what we have said. King moves effortlessly from quoting Scripture "… in the image of God …" to citing the Declaration "… all men are created equal…." And he calls this house of Scriptural stones and Declaration rafters, the American "home." That is what he meant in the great "I Have a Dream" speech when he told the multitude gathered before the Lincoln Memorial that his dream was, "deeply rooted in the American dream."

None of this should surprise the readers of this book by now. The conjunction of Biblical faith and natural reason that led to the Declaration gave it a religious significance so great that Samuel Adams was moved to say of the people's response to it: "[they] seem to recognize this resolution as though it were a decree promulgated from heaven." President Coolidge, in his Sesquicentennial address on the Declaration, had pointed out that "the principles of human relationship which went into the Declaration … are found in the … sermons and the writings of the early colonial clergy.… They preached equality because they believed in the fatherhood of God and the brotherhood of man. They justified freedom by the text that we are all created in the divine image, all partakers of the divine spirit." How strikingly similar this is to King's lament in *Where Do We Go from Here,* "We fail to think of them [men not of our own race or creed] as fellow human beings made from the same divine stuff as we are, molded in the same divine image."

KNIGHTS AND MARTYRS: Two Modes of Response to Jim Crow

Jews, Catholics, and Protestants were all prominent in the debates and demonstrations that led up to the Civil Rights Act of 1964. Perhaps a bit of reflection on the principal stances that the Judeo-Christian tradition has taken towards injustice will prove helpful here. We will characterize the religious citizen as martyr or knight, admittedly an overstatement, but one that may prove helpful.

The basic question is whether to "take up the sword." Recognizing as he does that injustice is not put right until the judgment or the coming of the Messiah, and that the wicked sometimes prosper, while the just suffer, what is the man of faith to do? One response is to seek personal perfection, suffer meekly, even unto death if necessary, and make one's own the love with which God loves even the sinner. Be ready to be a martyr. If you are not asked to give your life, you may have to sacrifice your career or your ambition. Do so patiently. Pray for the king, even in Babylon, and put away your sword. Make no alliance with Egypt, as Jeremiah taught, and become the faithful remnant. "He who lives by the sword shall die by the sword."

The other stance is, while praying to avoid the temptation to hate one's enemies, to stand up and fight for one's rights and people, trusting to Divine Judgment, but entering the fight. Of course, we are using the word "sword" chiefly metaphorically. We are not especially concerned with fighting to the death, but with political warfare, with the confrontation of demonstration and argument. Even without bloodshed, this kind of fighting can reduce friendship and civil concord and bring about personal and family strife that is most serious. Many American families saw that in the arguments here in our country about the Vietnam War, or about abortion, just as in the past town and clan were divided over slavery.

What made the martyr's course attractive in the decades after the Civil War was the end to be achieved. It was not only recognition in law and policy of the legal equality of the races that friends of the freedmen sought, but the civic and personal friendships, the genuine good will, that underlies a civil community. This required respect and affection, and respect and affection are sometimes better won by silence and deeds than by protests and demands. The name of Booker T. Washington is associated with this Christian choice of submissive and charitable patience and amity. The following is typical of his writings:

> The bedrock upon which every individual rests his chances of success in life is securing the friendship, the confidence, the respect, of his next door neighbor of the little community in which he lives.... There is at present no other safe course to

> pursue. If the Negro in the South has a friend in his white neighbor and a still larger number of friends in his community, he has a protection and a guarantee of his rights more potent and more lasting than any our Federal Congress or any outside power can confer.
> – *Booker T. Washington Papers* Volume 5: 1899–1900, ed. by Louis Harland & Raymond Smock, p. 191

As is this:

> If any white man would be mean, let us be good;
> if any white man would be little, let us be great;
> if any white man would push us down, let us push him up.
> If others can excel us in hating, let us excel them in loving.
> If others can excel us in cruelty, let us excel them in acts of mercy.
>
> You may call this cowardice; if so, it is the kind of cowardice that Christ taught and practiced, and it is the kind of cowardice that in the long run will win our cause.
> – *Ibid.*, p. 537

If these sentiments are not inconsistent with the dignity of man as taught in the Declaration, their omission or minimizing of the notion of "rights," makes them significantly different. Booker T. Washington thought that the strategy of raising up the black man by political defense of his rights in the Reconstruction had failed, and he also thought that he should order his life and the aspirations of his race to higher things, things that transcended politics. He would, and did, enter into political life quietly, backstage, as it were, to ameliorate the legal and social status of the black man, but he would lead no political crusade.

The way of the knight, defense of one's own rights and those of others, was signaled by a "Declaration of Principles" adopted in 1905 by a group called the "Niagara Movement." Many of the leaders and principles of the Niagara Movement were later incorporated in the National Association for the Advancement of Colored People (NAACP). Its most famous leader was

W.E.B. DuBois, whose career shows the power, and the temptations, of the knight's way. The following is taken from the "Declaration of Principles":

We note with alarm the evident retrogression in this land of sound public opinion on the subject of manhood rights, republican government and human brotherhood, and we pray God that this nation will not degenerate into a mob of boasters and oppressors, but rather will return to the faith of the fathers, that all men were created free and equal, with certain unalienable rights....

We refuse to allow the impression to remain that the Negro-American assents to inferiority, is submissive under oppression and apologetic before insults...

We urge upon Congress the enactment of appropriate legislation for securing the proper enforcement of those articles of freedom, the thirteenth, fourteenth, and fifteenth amendments of the Constitution of the United States....

The Negro race...needs justice, and is given charity, needs leadership, and is given cowardice and apology....

Of the above grievances, we do not hesitate to complain, and to complain loudly and insistently. To ignore, overlook, or apologize for these wrongs is to prove ourselves unworthy of our freedom. Persistent manly agitation is the way to liberty....

This statement, complaint, and prayer we submit to the American people and Almighty God.

– Taken from the *Declaration of Principles of the Niagara Movement*, 1905

There are three things that merit our attention in this "*Declaration of Principles.*" It looks to action, "persistent manly agitation" in the political arena. It explicitly cites Declaration principles. And it looks to "Almighty God," so much so that it terms itself both a complaint and a prayer.

This is the creed of a knight. It intends to make a fight. If the drawback in the martyr's way is that it may change nothing, that of the knight's is that he may lose his soul in the wasteland of pride and finally hate. Manly agitation may lead to manly pride, and then to sentiments like these from DuBois' later writings: "No race ever gave Passive resistance and Submission to Evil longer, more piteous trial. Today we raise the terrible weapon of self-defense … no human group has ever achieved freedom without being compelled to murder thousands of members of other groups who were determined that they should be slaves…." DuBois' personal vision of justice did not, in the end, include the principles of the Declaration, which he explicitly repudiated as "individualistic," nor did he rest in faith; he actually praised Joseph Stalin and held that a chief glory of Soviet socialism was the repression of religion, which he thought bred the passivity and submission he so despised. It was part of his political agenda to nurture the "memory of slavery" and the "experience of caste." John Hope Franklin, a writer not unfriendly to DuBois, reports that, "After seventy years of crusading for civil rights, W.E.B. Dubois had joined the Communist Party, renounced his United States citizenship, and moved to Ghana in 1961." DuBois died, two years later, an exile from his native land.

MARTIN LUTHER KING, JR.

Declaration statesmanship has been the theme of this chapter. The greatest instances of declaration statesmanship, the founding and the response to slavery, may be epitomized by the names of Jefferson and Lincoln. Of course they were aided (and opposed) by many men of talent and goodwill, and we would not be taken as saying that they alone stood like gods astride the concourse of history, determining events by their sovereign wills. Nor would we say that their every decision was wise or just. At the same time, their prudence and resolution changed the course of affairs, and we have tried to learn from them. We will conclude this chapter by making a similar effort with Martin Luther King, Jr.

Statesmen act in the real world, and their deeds are conditioned by what is actually possible. The founders faced the momentous task of establishing the first human government devoted to the propositions of natural right. They had a people on their side, and so it was proper for them, they argued, to revolutionize. They became the generals, congressmen, secretaries, and officers of that revolution and its government.

Lincoln faced the task of breathing new life into the founding principles when they were in danger of expiring. He foresaw that they would even be denied and trampled in the defense of slavery. His country chose him president because of his stance, founded in the Declaration, against slavery. After that time, he taught and reformed his country as its head of state. His triumph, which he paid for with his life, was the re-establishment and deepening of those principles.

For almost a century after Lincoln's death, those principles, though widely honored and accepted, had not been applied to all Americans. Some sophisticates in the academic world, indeed, denied them, but most Americans still cherished them while failing to apply them in the matter of race. Though this failure spread all over the country, and meant injustice for Asian-Americans, Mexican-Americans, American Indians and others, everyone knew that the case was worse for blacks in the South. The blacks themselves had tried Christian submission and political agitation, without making a fundamental change.

King was a preacher and a citizen, not an elected official. His cause was not, in the first instance, the cause of a nation, but of a racially distinct segment of that nation, only about 12% of the population. He and his movement had on their side the great moral prestige that Lincoln had reconquered for the Declaration, the legal provisions of the Fourteenth and Fifteenth Amendments, still largely paper guarantees, and the religious sensibilities of many of his fellow citizens. The black churches of the South, centers of education and community for more than a century, were a strong base of support. He also had a large number of whites of both parties who thought that Jim Crow was wrong, but who had not shown much strength or success in resisting it.

King could not operate from the seat of government, but he could take the higher ground of religion and moral principle. As a citizen, he could lead protest and discussion, and his allies could bring lawsuits. Since his cause was immediately in the interest of only one American in eight, he needed the goodwill of his fellow citizens; he needed to win their hearts and minds. Beyond this practical need, he wanted that goodwill, wanted it more than he wanted anything else. His dream was of human brotherhood, both as a Christian minister and as an American. In this, he was closer to Booker T. Washington than to the NAACP and Dubois. His own organization was called the Southern Christian Leadership Conference, and its motto was "To save the soul of America." He was a man of faith, and his horizon included more than politics. But even in politics, he knew that legal rights are grounded on human respect and friendship.

King's creative solution to the practical political problem was to force the evil in Jim Crow to show itself in the face of peaceful protest, engendering a non-hateful courage in his people and moderating the fears of those who fought with them. It was, when it worked, a wonderful blend of the knight and the martyr. It broke the spell of unmanliness in the Southern black, while it shielded protesters from the worst temptations to hatred and violence. National sympathy swung decisively to King's side when the dignified and brave protesters were arrested singing hymns and offering no physical resistance to the sheriff's men and their dogs.[20]

At the same time, he interpreted these feelings in accordance with religious and declaration thought, thereby ennobling them. He helped people to think about what they felt. The movement he led, and the moral success it obtained, enabled him to turn to politics and the law in a way that Booker T. Washington's earlier efforts could not. King said of the law, "[it] is a form of education. The words of the Supreme Court, of Congress, and of the Constitution are eloquent instructors." When President Kennedy was ready to ask Congress to pass what would become the Civil Rights Act of 1964, his words had been prepared by the labors of American statesmen from Jefferson to Lincoln to King:

> This nation was founded by men of many nations and backgrounds. It was founded on the principle that all men are created equal, and that the rights of every man are diminished when the rights of one man are threatened....
>
> We are confronted primarily with a moral issue. It is as old as the Scriptures and is as clear as the American Constitution....
>
> We have a right to expect that the Negro community will be responsible, will uphold the law, but they have a right to expect that law will be fair, that the Constitution will be color blind, as Justice Harlan said at the turn of the century.
>
> – President John F. Kennedy, *Address to the Nation*, June 11, 1963

When the Civil Rights Legislation that the President had called for passed in the two years after Kennedy's assassination, the people had every reason

20 https://www.pewresearch.org/fact-tank/2020/01/16/50-years-ago-mixed-views-about-civil-rights-but-support-for-selma-demonstrators/.

to believe that they had set an unalterable course to make their laws reflect the Declaration principle of equality, and the Judeo-Christian principle of brotherhood. No one could reasonably think that we had cured the ills of bigotry and pride in the human heart, but we had made a solemn commitment, as a people, to do what King had asked for in "I Have a Dream": to make a nation in which our children would be judged, "not by the color of their skin, but by the content of their character."

CHAPTER 10

A PEOPLE WORTHY OF THE DECLARATION

> "America, America, God mend thine every Flaw,
> Confirm thy Soul in Self-control, thy Liberty in Law"
> – *America the Beautiful,* second verse

Throughout this book we have attended to the subject of Declaration Statesmanship. Most of our statesmen, like the Founders or Lincoln, held high office. Others were non-official leaders like DuBois and King. But it is to be kept in mind that ours is a government "of the people." So, though each and every citizen need not hold office, still in some sense, each rules the republic, together with his fellows.

The Constitution opens, "We the People...." Ours is a popular government, a republic. We think it proper, accordingly, to consider what kind of people, with what loves and what virtues, can live out declaration principles. To this subject, we now turn.

> The nations of our time cannot prevent the conditions of men from becoming equal, but it depends upon themselves whether the principle of equality is to lead them to servitude or freedom, to knowledge or barbarism, to prosperity or wretchedness.
> – Alexis de Tocqueville, *Democracy in America,* final sentence

In 1831, 55 years after the Declaration of Independence and 42 years after the adoption of the Constitution, a young French nobleman came to visit America. His name was Alexis de Tocqueville. Although of noble birth, the young Tocqueville was a friend of democracy. Democracy, however, had not had a happy history in France. The French Revolution of 1789, although founded on some of the same principles as the American Revolution (notably not, however, acknowledgment of the Creator as the source of human rights) had never attained stability. Violent struggles for power among its leaders culminated in the elevation of an emperor, Napoleon. After Napoleon's fall, the French were governed by unstable monarchical regimes, the first under a restored House of Bourbon, and the next headed by the so-called "citizen king," Louis Philippe.

Democratic ideals did not die under the restored monarchy, and Tocqueville believed that the power of the idea of equality would make some form of democracy the government of the future for all Western countries. But he was troubled by the lack of political stability and the tendency toward tyranny that France's first democratic efforts had shown. Similar problems were experienced in Central and South America, where the former Spanish colonies had been unable to establish stable, peaceful popular rule. Many others in Europe held a more pessimistic view than Tocqueville. They believed that ordinary people could never rule themselves, and would always be prey to enterprising, ruthless men promising them the stability of dictatorial rule. They argued that only a king or an aristocracy, a small group of men who were trained to rule and entitled to do so by birth, could provide stable, peaceful government for a country.

Amidst the turbulent sea of floundering democracies, the United States rose up like an island of refuge. For over half a century, the people of the United States, and the millions of immigrants who had joined them, had managed to rule themselves successfully. Democracy in America had prospered and expanded. Tocqueville came to America hoping to discover the secrets of its success, some of which might help to guide France and other European countries on their road to democratic rule.

Tocqueville concluded that neither the natural advantages of the land nor the written constitution were sufficient to explain America's peace, stability and prosperity. Instead, he thought that these goods came from what he called her customs, what we might call the character or the culture of the people.

> The customs of the Americans of the United States are, then, the peculiar cause which renders that people the only one of the American nations that is able to support a democratic government.... I am convinced that the most advantageous situation

> and the best possible laws cannot maintain a constitution in spite of the customs of a country; while the latter may turn to some advantage the most unfavorable positions and the worst laws.
> – *Democracy in America,* Vol. I, p. 334

What Tocqueville means by "customs" (the French word is "*moeurs*") he tells us in several places, one of which is perhaps the most concise and illuminating. He writes in a footnote:

> I understand by this word the sum of the intellectual and moral dispositions that men bring to the state of society.

In this book we use the more ordinary English word, "character" to express the same idea.

In this chapter, we will investigate the customs that have made our country the most successful democracy in history. We will also look at the cultural tendencies that currently threaten our form of government, and ask ourselves the question: Are we still a People with the character required for genuine Freedom?

If you try to imagine living in the early days of the United States, you might feel yourself separated from your forefathers by a great gulf. Our life today is so bound up with modern conveniences that make home and work far easier, if not simpler—cars, cell phones, refrigerators, electric lights, computers, the internet. Entertainment is a major part of everyday life—TV shows, movies, stereos, restaurants. To say nothing of social media! As I edit this text on my word processor, I have a classical music station playing, and Facebook open!

Most of us live in or near large cities. We can fly to Europe or Asia fairly easily, and have friends all over America, and in other nations as well. In these respects, daily life in late eighteenth century America was unlike ours, but much like that of most generations of men that had come before it. Closer to the farm and small town, slower and with fewer forms of entertainment. What made Americans different from their contemporaries in other countries?

SELF-GOVERNMENT

Perhaps the most important difference between the early Americans and the Spanish who formed the next modern republics was their experience in being free. When historians search for the roots of the ideals of liberty that informed the Declaration of Independence, they often begin with the Magna Carta of 1215, the document that forced the English king to acknowledge certain rights of the nobles. Over the next five hundred years, with many ups and downs, the English people gradually attained greater liberties and more of a role in government. Through a series of conflicts with the king, Parliament gained greater responsibility, including the power to control the amount of money raised in the form of taxes. This gave the representatives in the House of Commons, whose members were chosen from among the non-aristocratic segments of society, experience in making the laws of the land.

As we noted above, this experience in self-government increased in British America long before the Revolution. For various reasons, no aristocracy had ever been established in the American colonies. The colonists were permitted by their charters from the king (which authorized them to settle the land claimed by the Crown) to form their own governments. The popularly-elected colonial assemblies did not have to share power with an aristocracy, as the House of Commons in Britain did.

For 150 years, these assemblies, with the approval of governors, generally appointed by the king, enacted nearly all the legislation necessary for the colonies. As old Captain Preston said, "We had always ruled ourselves." And, as his taking up his musket proved, we loved the liberty we had experienced.

Because there was no aristocracy, the colonists gained valuable experience in freedom in another way a wider sense. Under aristocratic rule, the noblemen owned much of the land in England, while commoners were often tenants on the lord's property. In the colonies, ownership of property was more widely diffused. Workmen owned the tools they employed in their trades. Most farmers owned the land they farmed. Other colonists owned small workshops or merchant ships. Most colonists were used to the responsibility that comes with ownership. They knew the risks that come with property, and they also knew the profit that comes with managing it diligently and intelligently. They learned how to associate with others with similar goals, to share resources to achieve more. All these exercises in freedom required self-control. Accordingly, these early Americans were, in one sense, quite independent before Independence.

Life in those times was very difficult, and not only in America. Each family had to work hard to thrive, sometimes just to survive. And they found that they could do it, to a great degree, by self-control, without help from nobles, Parliament, or even their own colonial assemblies. But in another sense, they were quite *inter*dependent. Tocqueville notes that only by common efforts could Americans compensate for the lack of an aristocracy.

> Aristocratic communities always contain, among a multitude of persons who by themselves are powerless, a small number of powerful and wealthy citizens, each of whom can achieve great undertakings single-handed....
>
> Among democratic nations, on the contrary, all the citizens are independent and feeble; they can do hardly anything by themselves, and none of them can oblige his fellow men to lend him their assistance. They all, therefore, become powerless if they do not learn voluntarily to help one another.
>
> – *Democracy in America*, Vol II, p. 11

Americans became masters of voluntary association. They combined to found a school or a college, to set up a volunteer fire company, or to pitch in and help other families in difficulty without the command of a magistrate or sheriff. According to Tocqueville, Americans offered such help not only from charity, but also because they thought it in their own interest. They knew that the time would likely come when they also would need help or they saw the increase of learning and morality as beneficial to them in the long run. All this continued after 1776 and into the first half century of the new republic, when Tocqueville came to visit and observe America.

Our forefathers were thus self-governing in two distinct, but related senses. They were largely independent owners of property, which they governed according to their own good sense, and they were also experienced in forming and sustaining self-governing associations so as to overcome their isolation and individual weakness, and to receive aid from others when they might need it. Both kinds of self-government required and fostered prudence and submission of appetite to reason. Self-government in associations also developed habits of lawfulness and compromise, and experience of the rules of debate and decision making.

These habits and experiences were vital to the experiment in full political self-government that the Declaration would inaugurate. They were also crucial to the design of limited government set out in the Constitution, since it was only by the capacity of the people in voluntary associations to conduct affairs in business, the arts, religion, and education, that these affairs could be managed apart from government, and in particular, centralized government. Tocqueville put the last point this way:

> Nothing, in my opinion, is more deserving of our attention than the intellectual and moral associations of America. The political and industrial associations of that country strike us forcibly; but the others elude our observation, or if we discover them, we understand them imperfectly because we have hardly ever seen anything of the kind. It must be acknowledged, however, that they are as necessary to the American people as the former, and perhaps more so. In democratic countries the science of association is the mother of science; the progress of all the rest depends upon the progress it has made.
> – *Democracy in America*, Vol. II, p. 118

America has been called the country of individual rights and individualism. The reason for the first is that the inalienable rights of the Declaration belong to the individual, not to groups, such as ethnic or racial groups, or to clans, or societies. They are the rights of man.

Naturally, then, we tend to be "individualists" and to prize individualism. Tocqueville, who was an admirer of America, who seems to have invented the term, gives a definition of individualism followed it, together with a sharp criticism of it. He writes:

> Individualism is a mature and calm feeling, which disposes each member of the community to sever himself from the mass of

> his fellows and to draw apart with his family and his friends, so that after he has thus formed a little circle of his own, he willingly leaves society at large to itself.... [Individualism makes] every man forget his ancestors ... it hides his descendants and separates his contemporaries from him; it throws him back forever upon himself alone and threatens in the end to confine him entirely within the solitude of his own heart.
> – *Democracy in America*, Vol. II, p. 104 & 106

Can you see why self-government as discussed above might be a remedy for these terrible consequences of unchecked individualism? Tocqueville looks to civic and political associations, and what he calls, "the principle of self-interest rightly understood" to combat these evils. We will return to the problem of individualism in the next section.

COURAGE AND PRUDENCE

> "Don't Tread on Me!"
> – Motto on 'rattlesnake flag' designed by Christopher Gadsden, 1775

The following thoughts on a rattlesnake are attributed to Ben Franklin:

> I recollected that her eye excelled in brightness, that of any other animal, and that she has no eye-lids—She may therefore be esteemed an emblem of vigilance.—She never begins an attack, nor, when once engaged, ever surrenders: She is therefore an emblem of magnanimity and true courage.—As if anxious to prevent all pretensions of quarreling with her, the weapons with which nature has furnished her, she conceals in the roof of her mouth, so that, to those who are unacquainted with her, she appears to be a most defenseless animal; and even when those weapons are shown and extended for her defense, they appear weak and contemptible; but their wounds however small, are decisive and fatal:—Conscious of this, she never wounds till she has generously given notice, even to her enemy, and cautioned him against the danger of stepping on her.—Was I wrong, Sir,

> in thinking this a strong picture of the temper and conduct of America?

In 1775 the rattlesnake found its way onto one of the first American flags, the bright yellow Gadsden Flag, over the words, "Don't Tread on Me." Roughly a year and a half later, the rattlesnake was officially adopted by the Continental Congress to serve as the nation's first symbol, approving the design for the official Seal of the War Office. Today, the rattlesnake is still included in the design of the Department of the Army's official seal.[21]

The nation founded on the Declaration depends for its existence on a thirst for independence. This thirst must be so strong that it is worth dying for. It must be the grounds for courage. Is it an accident that the National Anthem, the "Star Spangled Banner," ends with the phrase, "the land of the free and the home of the brave?" Because freedom entails both risking yourself and taking care of yourself, it is not the easiest way to live. In many ways, it is much easier never to put yourself on the firing line, and to have someone else take care of you and make all the important decisions.

So the man worthy of freedom must first of all desire it above lower goods—more than pleasure, than ease, than excitement, than security. This makes him into a man of moral courage. He will not fail to take responsibility for his actions because he knows that is the mark of a free man. President Harry Truman was widely known for his motto, "The Buck Stops Here." When decisions he made turned out for the worse, he didn't want to blame it on anyone else, because that would have meant he was not responsible for his own actions. Even his political opponents had to admire this feature of his character.

But desire isn't enough. To want to take care of yourself and to be willing to take responsibility for your actions will only do harm if you always make bad decisions. A young man who falls in with a local gang and winds up in prison might admit that he was responsible for his fate, but he has wasted much of his life. So has a woman who finds herself in a relationship with a man who abuses her, cheats on her and then abandons her. Or the head of a family who entrusts their inheritance to swindlers. Even if they all accept the consequences, they have still erred, and erred grossly.

21 http://militaryinsignia.blogspot.com/2010/07/united-states-army-seal.html.

Independence requires the ability to make sound judgments, in addition to the willingness to stand behind one's judgments. Traditionally, the steady capacity of making good decisions was known as prudence. It comes from good education, experience, and heeding the advice of the wise.

POLITICAL FREEDOM

So far we have talked about what makes a man capable of taking care of himself. In America, freedom has a more profound meaning, because adults not only take care of themselves and their families, they also have a role to play in caring for their community, state and country.

The freedom that our founders fought for was the right to participate in making laws for themselves, in deciding what their taxes should be used for, in choosing their chief executives and legislators, in applying the laws, in short, what we have called "self-government." We still enjoy this freedom, which we usually exercise by voting for people to represent us and by serving on juries. That means that, in this country, we are the rulers. *We* are "Caesar." Just as everything done by an ambassador is done by authority of the president, everything done in our city, state or country is done on our authority.

With this kind of liberty comes a new level of responsibility. Because we are the rulers, we have to be able to make good decisions for the whole community. We have to stay informed about important issues, and about how our representatives are performing in office. We also need to participate in the public discussions that will play an important role in determining what decisions are made. The demands such civic participation makes on our time and understanding should not be taken lightly, particularly in view of the temptations of "individualism."

To do our civic duty well requires that we love it and work at it, just as with any other duty. And that work involves getting and understanding a good deal of information. This is one reason that the founding generation believed in limiting the national government. The further away from us decisions were made, the harder it was for us to participate in them intelligently. Any member can go to a local Rotary Club or Labor Union meeting and have his say. Today, participation in local civic and political and religious groups is accessible to us all, as are local school board or city council meetings.

And so, thanks to the internet, are many other modes of common action and deliberation. But if all the important decisions are usurped by judges and bureaucrats, or made in unresponsive and antiquated state capitals or in Washington, D.C., we will have little say in what laws govern the place where we live.

EDUCATION

> It is in republican government that the full power of education is needed. Fear in despotic governments arises of itself from threats and chastisements; honor in monarchies is favored by the passions and favors them in turn; but political virtue is a renunciation of oneself, which is always a very painful thing.
>
> One can define this virtue as love of the laws and the homeland. This love, requiring a continuous preference of the public interest over ones own, produces all the individual virtues; they are only that preference.
>
> This love is singularly connected with democracies. In them alone, government is entrusted to each citizen. Now government is like all things in the world; in order to preserve it, one must love it....
>
> ... Therefore, in a republic, everything depends on establishing this love, and education should attend to inspiring it.
>
> – Montesquieu, *Spirit of the Laws*, Part 1, Bk 4, ch.5

> ... no sort of comparison can be drawn between the pioneer and the dwelling that shelters him. Everything about him is primitive and wild, but he is himself the result of the labor and experience of eighteen centuries. He wears the dress and speaks the language of cities; he is acquainted with the past, curious about the future, and ready for argument about the present; he is, in short, a highly civilized being, who consents for a time to inhabit the backwoods, and who penetrates into the wilds of the New World with the Bible, an axe, and some newspapers.
>
> – *Democracy in America*, Vol. I p. 328

"What I do with my own life" always affects other people. This is especially true in a democracy, where each one of us bears in a particular way the responsibility of making decisions that affect all. To do this well, we need to have the moral character to take that responsibility seriously. But we also need to have an education that allows us to discern what is truly best.

In monarchies, attention was given to the education of the heir who eventually would rule the people, making decisions affecting the whole nation. In a democracy, the students in our public and private schools, and in their homes, are the heirs. They will soon have a role in determining the direction our communities, our state, our nation will take. Students who prefer feeling to reflection or prejudice to reason will not make good decisions. Some appreciation of this truth has consistently led Americans to endeavor to include some amount of character formation in our common schools. And that formation is often recollected with gratitude to the beloved teachers or coaches who have changed and shaped our lives.

We certainly need schools where traits of good character are supported and even encouraged. But a good heart without a clear head is blind. To act well, to achieve good, a good hearted American student needs to *understand* the principles that have made his country. Since these principles stem from the two primary lights of western civilization, Natural and Divine Law, it will be well for our students to come to know books of Plato and Moses, the researches of Aristotle, the orations of Cicero, the teachings of Socrates and St. Paul, in short the prime students of Nature, and the prime students of Nature's God. That is, something of what is called "Liberal Education" is essential for the free man. American students in particular must also come to know the great figures of our own republic, men in whose lives our principles shine.

Tocqueville considered the Americans to be as a whole the most enlightened nation in the history of the world. With the exception of slaves, who were generally, though not universally, illiterate, almost no American was without a basic education. While most Americans didn't proceed to a study of philosophy or the fine arts, they did understand the history of their country, its forms of government and its laws. Through their formal education, their newspapers, their conversations, and, above all else, their participation in government, Americans understood the fundamental rights described in the Declaration of Independence, and how their laws, their customs and their forms of government were arranged to maintain those rights.

> The American learns to know the laws by participating in the act of legislation; and he takes a lesson in the forms of government from governing.
> – *Democracy in America*, Vol. I

Tocqueville, however, was not an uncritical observer. He also points out that, up to the 1830's our literature was scanty, our theoretical science of little value, and our philosophers non-existent. With melancholy reluctance, Tocqueville concluded that there would never be in America such a soul as a Blaise Pascal, the greatest Christian inquirer he knew of. An observer of the state of learning in America, he says, "must consider the same object from two different points of view. If he singles out only the learned, he will be astonished to find out how few they are; but if he counts the ignorant, the American people will appear to be the most enlightened in the world."

On the other hand, Morrison, describing the education of the founding generation, in the *Oxford History,* speaks of the "sound education in the ancient classics and political theory that young men obtained at the College of William and Mary." He adds, "running a plantation, serving on the council or in the house of burgesses, and reading Cicero, Polybius, and Locke gave Virginians an excellent training in statesmanship."

Perhaps this difference between authors can be traced to the periods they have in mind. The Liberal Education of the 18th Century Virginians and others that Morrison refers to was an inheritance from English and European tradition, and in some measure aristocratic. The American of Tocqueville's time was much more the frontiersman and democrat of the days of Davy Crockett and Andrew Jackson. Democracy had, in some measure, pushed aside common liberal learning, and replaced it with self-instruction or with the useful. Moral instruction continued of course, in the elementary school. One only need look at the McGuffey Readers to see that. But the higher learning was then, and seems always to be, in some peril in America.

Tocqueville thought that we Americans compensated for our lack of "book-learning" by political and social practice.

> It cannot be doubted that in the United States the instruction of the people powerfully contributes to the support of the democratic republic; and such must always be the case, I believe, where the instruction which enlightens the understanding is not separated from the moral education which amends the heart. But I would not exaggerate this advantage, and I am still further from thinking, as so many people do think in Europe, that men can be instantaneously made citizens by teaching them how to read and write. True information is mainly derived from experience; and if the Americans had not been gradually accustomed to govern themselves, their book-learning would not help them much at the present day.
> – *Democracy in America*, Vol. I, p. 329

But Americans did connect primary education with self-government in Tocqueville's day, and they made the case for higher education as well. The University of Virginia was a beloved project of Jefferson, and his so called "Rockfish Gap" Report of 1818 sketched the public purposes of both primary and higher education. About the first he wrote,

> The objects of ... primary education [which] determine its character and limits [are]: To give to every citizen the information he needs for the transaction of his own business; to enable him to calculate for himself, and to express and preserve his ideas, his contracts and accounts in writing; to improve, by reading, his morals and faculties; to understand his duties to his neighbors and country, and to discharge with competence the functions confided to him by either; to know his rights; to exercise with order and justice those he retains, to choose with discretion the fiduciary of those he delegates; and to notice their conduct with diligence, with candor and judgment; and in general, to observe with intelligence and faithfulness all the social relations under which he shall be placed.

As to higher education:

> [the purpose of the public institutions of higher learning is] …
> To form the statesmen, legislators, and judges, on whom public prosperity and individual happiness are so much to depend …
> To develop the reasoning faculties of our youth, enlarge their minds, cultivate their morals, and instill into them the precepts of virtue and order;
> … And, generally, to form them to habits of reflection and correct action, rendering them examples of virtue to others, and of happiness to themselves.
> – *Report of the Commissioners of the University of Virginia*, August 4, 1818, (drafted by Thomas Jefferson)

The report on the plans for the University of Virginia, quoted above, makes for fascinating reading. One thing that strikes us is Jefferson's omission of theological and scriptural studies. He explains this omission as proceeding "… in conformity with the principles of our [Virginia's]Constitution which places all sects of religion on an equal footing, with the jealousies of the different sects in guarding that equality, and with the sentiments of the Legislature in favor of freedom of religion…." But he goes on to add that "proofs of the being of a God" will be presented in the Ethics courses, and he speaks of this God in language that takes one back to the Declaration; He is the source of the moral law and hence of political justice and all moral obligations, and is our maker and ruler. But there will be no professor of divinity, and no teaching of the contents of scripture as sacred. He also says nothing of theoretical philosophy, and his only mention of mathematics and physics quickly links those studies to advances in medicine and technological applications. Jefferson himself could, and did, read Homer in the original Greek, but he does not praise the classics, though Latin, Hebrew, and Greek [and Anglo-Saxon!] are among the studies listed by name later in the report, with the brief remark that these languages are "the foundation common to all the sciences." Presumably this has something to do with their roles as the sources of many words in the modern languages, a reason commonly given today for the study of Latin. The notion of the useful dominates that of the contemplative throughout. And he has bitter words for the backwards-looking universities of Europe, with their close bonds to the churches. Political philosophy, though, a central element in the ideal of liberal education from the time of Plato, is present, as we have noted.

Jefferson's university was unique, however, in its hostility to revelation. Nearly all our institutions of higher learning began as seminaries, and continued to include a strong religious element for decades after the founding of the University of Virginia. And some of them were also explicit in their devotion to what we would call liberal education as well. A famous document in our educational history, issued from a committee of Yale College in 1828, argues thus:

> As in our primary schools, reading, writing, and arithmetic are taught to all, however different their prospects; so in a college, all should be instructed in those branches of knowledge, of which no one destined to the higher walks of life ought to be ignorant. What subject which is now studied here, could be set aside, without evidently marring the system? Not to speak particularly, in this place, of the ancient languages; who that aims at a well proportioned and superior education will remain ignorant of the elements of the various branches of the mathematics, or of history and antiquities, or of rhetoric and oratory, or natural philosophy, or astronomy, or chemistry, or mineralogy, or geology, or political economy, or mental and moral philosophy?

Returning briefly to primary education, note that the same "Rockfish Gap" report summarizes the purposes of the common schools of Virginia as instructing all its youth in their "rights, interests, and duties, as men and citizens." Jefferson takes particular notice of "discretion" in the choice of those to whom our rights are delegated, that is, to public officials, and he lays stress on the students' knowing their rights and improving their morals. As one might expect, for Jefferson, this moral aim is not closely tied to sectarian belief. But in much of the rest of America, that tie was stronger. Tocqueville remarks of the public schools in the America of the 1830's: "The greater part of education is entrusted to the clergy" (page 283) and Morrison, writing of the Colonial schools in New England writes: "The religious sentiment was basic" (page 71). All of these schools, of course, started with "reading, writing, and arithmetic." We have paid special attention to their moral, political, and religious aspects, since our inquiry concerns the character of our forebears.

As we have seen before, Lincoln has a way of getting at the kernel of his countrymen's ways. So it is with education. When he first ran for the state legislature in Illinois in 1832, he issued a "Political Announcement" in which he set out his views on local affairs. The following paragraph from the "Political Announcement" gives his stance on education:

> Upon the subject of education, not presuming to dictate any plan or system respecting it, I can only say that I view it as the most important subject which we as a people can be engaged in. That every man may receive at least, a moderate education, and thereby be enabled to read the histories of his own and other countries, by which he may duly appreciate the value of our free institutions, appears to be an object of vital importance, even on this account alone, to say nothing of the advantages and satisfaction to be derived from all being able to read the scriptures and other works, both of a religious and moral nature, for themselves. For my part, I desire to see the time when education, and by its means, morality, sobriety, enterprise and industry, shall become much more general than at present, and should be gratified to have it in my power to contribute something to the advancement of any measure which might have a tendency to accelerate the happy period.

RELIGION

> "Our fathers' God to thee, author of Liberty, to thee we sing."
> – *My Country, 'tis of thee*, final stanza

> When [friends of republican government] attack religious opinions, they obey the dictates of their passions and not of their interests. Despotism may govern without faith, but liberty cannot. Religion is much more necessary in the republic which they set forth in glowing colors than in the monarchy which they

> attack; it is more needed in democratic republics than in any others. How is it possible that society should escape destruction if the moral tie is not strengthened in proportion as the political tie is relaxed? And what can be done with a people who are their own masters if they are not submissive to the Deity?
>
> – *Democracy in America*, Vol. I, Part Two, ch. 9

> Religion in America takes no direct part in the government of society, but it must be regarded as the first of their political institutions....
>
> – *Democracy in America*, Vol. I, Part Two, ch. 10

Men and women of our times will sometimes say that there is no public role for religion in American life. Belief in God or lack of it, they say, is merely a private matter; it makes, or ought to make, no difference to our public institutions. Ideological lobbies pushing this view, such as *People for the American Way*, cite the First Amendment and its interpretation by the Supreme Court in such matters as public school prayer and holiday displays to show that religion has no legitimate place in public life.

This was not the view of Americans at the time of the Declaration, or at the time when the religious liberty provisions of the First Amendment were adopted. As Supreme Court Justice Joseph Story put it a generation after the founding, "... piety, religion, and morality are intimately connected with the well-being of the state.... The promulgation of the great doctrines of religion ... can never be a matter of indifference in any well-ordered community."

And the Americans of those days were, on the whole, pious men. Most of them practiced a religion, generally some form of Protestant Christianity, and even those who did not recognized its crucial importance for the success of the democratic experiment.

In fact, the First Amendment to the Constitution was proposed, in part, as a way to *encourage* the influence of religious belief on people. In the House debates on its ratification, Daniel Carroll, a Roman Catholic from Maryland, said in passing, in his argument for adoption, that it was backed by "many sects." Madison, who held a stronger view in favor of the separation of church and state than did many of the other founders, took notice of the effects of the religious liberty established by the founding generation in 1819, by remarking with pleasure that "there has been an increase of religious instruction since the revolution."

By preventing the national government from becoming identified with one religious sect, the First Amendment served two functions. It prevented people of differing religious beliefs from being persecuted by governmental power directed to one religious body at the expense of the others. Thus it kept the union free from becoming a slave of a religious sect. It also prevented religion from becoming a tool of political power, an abuse that Madison called, "an unhallowed perversion of the means of salvation."

Within two generations, all the states had similar religious liberty provisions in their constitutions. Before that time, there had been more or less effective, and more or less oppressive, establishment of religion in the American colonies and states. But in Europe, where most countries still had established state religions, many people lost their faith when they saw Christianity serving tyranny and oppression, or by its wielding state power to persecute believers of other sects. This was especially scandalous for American Christians who saw the laws of the Old World used to persecute other Christians, and for men of goodwill, including unbelievers, who recoiled from the horrors of the religious wars in Europe and England. Indeed, some leading writers of the European "Enlightenment," including, in his later career, our own Thomas Paine, considered religious faith to be an enemy to freedom and knowledge.

But the early Americans knew from experience that some religious faith was essential to free institutions. One reason for this view is obvious. Where men are free to do anything, they will always be tempted to use their power to commit injustice against others. In America, where the desire of the majority could always be made into law and enforced on others, the temptation to seize the property or liberty of the minority was always present. No benevolent monarch, no kindly lord, stood ready to protect the few people from the many.

With such unlimited power, only the people could restrain themselves from injustice. Reverence for God and His laws taught Americans the limits within which they could use their unlimited power. American children were schooled in the Ten Commandments, and in the Gospel injunction, "Do unto others as you would have them do unto you."

And so, without direct establishment, American public opinion, always the deepest and most powerful force in our republic, strongly supported religion. Whatever the secrets of their own hearts, American statesmen, even the freethinking Jefferson, patronized religion. Statesmen and citizens alike felt that men whose consciences are formed according to religious precepts are more able to govern themselves wisely, and less likely to abuse their power. The near-universal acceptance of common religious moral teaching made it more possible for one man to trust the decency or justice of another. Washington made a similar point in his *Farewell Address* when he asked,

> Where is the security for property, for reputation, for life, if the sense of religious obligation *desert* the oaths which are the instruments of investigation in courts of justice?

The solemnity of a religious oath, made with the hand on the Bible, makes a pious soul less likely to bear false witness. Of course, Christianity or Judaism did not perfectly restrain men from treating one another unjustly, and gravely unjustly, too, as we have seen in the case of slavery. But the moral ideals implanted by faith in God were powerful helps in preventing, in hindering, and even in reversing grievous errors. Where is your money, your child, your life, and your own soul safer, at a rock concert, a movie, a public street, on the one hand, or on the other, at worship in a church or synagogue? All are filled with sinners, but in the church and synagogue since you are more likely to be flanked by those who admit they are sinners and strive to be better—for they know "the just man sins seven times a day" (Proverbs 24:16)—so too are you likely to strive for an upright life.

That these ideals were more or less agreed upon, while the mysteries and transcendental aspects of faith were left outside the public sphere meant that some of the most exalted things, the things that command the deepest loyalties in men, were not subjects of political division. This had a much needed pacifying effect on our politics, insulating us against the sectarian savagery seen all too often on this globe.

> ... if any hold that the religious spirit which I admire is the very thing most amiss in America, and that the only element wanting

to the freedom and happiness of the human race on the other side of the ocean [is the replacement of God by nature or scientific materialism], I can only reply that those who hold this language have never been in America and that they have never seen a religious or a free nation. When they return from a visit to that country [America], we shall hear what they have to say.
– Tocqueville, *Democracy in America*, Vol. I, Part Two, ch. 1

CHAPTER 11

DANGERS TO FREEDOM IN OUR TIME

> At what point then is the approach of danger to be expected? I answer, if it ever reach us, it must spring up amongst us. It cannot come from abroad. If destruction be our lot, we must ourselves be its author and finisher. As a nation of freemen, we must live through all time, or die by suicide.
> – Abraham Lincoln, Lyceum speech, January 27, 1838

A FALSE IDEA OF FREEDOM

At no time in our country's history have we been a nation of unstained righteousness. Not even the generation that founded our nation met the demands of authentic freedom, most notably in the case of slavery. Nor did those who came after the crisis of the Civil War. And yet, the noble idea of the free man was always present. Even when we didn't meet its demands of self-control, responsibility, and respect for natural rights, we honored the idea in our homilies and speeches. Our idea showed corruptions and injustices in their true colors; it rallied us in time of national trial. Throughout our history, it has shown its great power to reform, to call our nation back to its founding principles.

Today, however, it is the very idea of freedom which is under attack. We saw in the last section that freedom demands responsibility. But we are all aware that a very different understanding of what it means to be free permeates our society. According to this view, freedom means more than making our own decisions; it means not having anyone tell us that we should behave any differently. In this view, no teacher, no parent, no governor, no preacher, not even God Himself has the right to tell a person what he should do.

This specious view, which takes freedom to be license to do anything at all, makes self-governing undesirable and finally impossible. The more we indulge our desires, the less interested we become in making the effort to live according to reason. The man of passion may look strong and free on the outside, but inside he is personally and politically weak.

What might our political future be if we succumb to this false dream of freedom? Like a self-indulgent monarch who turns all the state's affairs over to a Grand Vizier only too eager for the power, and finds himself the slave of his former servant, we could continue to give more of our authority to our magistrates so that we too might indulge ourselves. As long as our leaders continued to flatter and pamper us, we would continue to increase their power. If those in positions of power also believed freedom equaled license, they would have no reason not to use their power to fulfill their own desires, as long as they could get away with it. The more power they have, the more they will be able to get away with. They would become tyrants. And we would wake up one day to find that we had become slaves.

This is the pattern that republics all too often follow. In the last years of the Roman Republic, ordinary citizens were happy to give power to ambitious men who promised to feed and entertain them. The Roman authors even had a phrase for it: "*panem et circenses*"—"bread and circuses." Julius Caesar, Pompey, Mark Anthony, and other glamorous and ambitious men then used their influence to satisfy their own desires and increase their power. Defenders of the Republic, like Cato and Cicero, were swept aside; civil disorders and political murders multiplied; the honest suffered and the unscrupulous prospered. The corruption in both citizens and officials became so great that most were thankful when Augustus finally subjected everyone to his own supreme authority, in what the historians call, "the Peace of Augustus."

The relatively mild Augustus was then followed by his grim nephew, Tiberius, and by such horrors as Caligula and Nero. How terrible was the peace of Augustus, we may read in Tacitus' *Annals*. Virtue, in Tacitus' narrative, is so rare that upon meeting it we are surprised before we are delighted.

The partisans of license betray authentic freedom in two other ways. First, they deny the natural law, and maintain that what is evil is either good or neutral. Finding this difficult to defend to others or even to be believed by themselves, and wishing to justify their uncontrolled behavior in some particular arena, they find themselves tempted to deny that human beings can control their actions more generally. "Our behavior is determined," they are led to believe, "by our genes and hormones, by our upbringing, by oppressive social structures." The poor are now expected to steal; those of a group abused by the policeman, to riot. Teenagers can't control their sexual drives, ambitious types can't help lying and stepping on others, angry people can't help being abusive. What are in fact moral problems are treated as physical illnesses or addictions or weaknesses no one can be expected to resist.

We can see this clearly in the recent history of the drive to legitimize homosexual behavior. When homosexual "rights" first became an issue, proponents argued that all men are free to make their own choices. Since, they argued, homosexual acts giving sexual pleasure were morally neutral, or even good, and to discriminate against homosexuality was to punish an acceptable use of freedom. Then, in an almost complete contradiction of this argument, they made another, denying that it was a free choice at all. They said that some people are born homosexuals. Their genetic make-up forces them into their homosexual "lifestyle." So to discriminate against such people is just like discriminating against people of different races. A white or black man can't help the color of his skin; a homosexual can't help his preordained lifestyle. And this person must not suffer any sign of public disapprobation. The sexual partnership with another of the same sex must be open to the title of marriage, for instance.

But this sort of argument makes freedom both impossible and dangerous. If this argument is true, why should it not apply to other kinds of behavior? People born with bad tempers, with propensities to lie or steal, with a taste for sexual relations with children, can't be expected to control themselves. Of course, these last examples rather plainly involve the public good. Accordingly, we are now faced with a policy question. What shall we do? When someone can't control actions dangerous for society, then his ability to act in those ways must be either curtailed or tolerated. We end in either license or repression. Plato foresaw this centuries before our time. Here he has Socrates speak with a young Athenian citizen. Socrates speaks first:

> ... "[since they cannot put up with obedience in any way, thinking it slavery, the members of the democratic city] end up, as you well know, by paying no attention to the laws, written or

> unwritten, in order that they may avoid having any master at all."
>
> "Of course, I know it," he said.
>
> "Well, then, my friend," I said, "this is the beginning … from which tyranny in my opinion naturally grows."
>
> – Plato, *Republic*, Book VIII, 563 e

UNDERMINING MARRIAGE AND THE FAMILY

> There is certainly no country in the world where the tie of marriage is more respected than in America or where conjugal happiness is more highly or worthily appreciated. In Europe, almost all the disturbances of society arise from the irregularities of domestic life…. But when the American retires from the turmoil of public life to the bosom of his family, he finds in it the image of order and of peace. There his pleasures are simple and natural, his joys are innocent and calm; and as he finds that an orderly life is the surest path to happiness, he accustoms himself easily to moderate his opinions as well as his tastes. While the European endeavors to forget his domestic troubles by agitating society, the American derives from his own home that love of order which he afterwards carries with him into public affairs.
>
> –Tocqueville, *Democracy in America*, Vol. 1, Part Two, ch.10

Today, the traditional family is under stress as never before. Our tax laws and social legislation encourage mothers to hand over the care of children to governmental agencies, our divorce rates are much higher than in the past, the police have their hands full tracking down "deadbeat dads," illegitimate births are at shockingly high levels, and the very notion of a normal family, consisting of two adults, a man and a woman, united in marriage, and their children, is questioned.

When family life fails, so do the strong moral habits that make the exercise of freedom in public life possible. Within the family, parents learn how to care for others. They learn to think beyond the present moment, because they have to plan for the future of their children and grandchildren.

The effort to keep their marriage vows schools husband and wife in the habits of controlling passion and keeping promises. Children learn how to control their own actions from the example, instruction and discipline of their parents. Even value-free social studies confirm that children raised *outside* of the marriage-based, two-parent family have worse chances in life, greater incidence of crime and drug addiction, lower grades in school, higher rates of poverty and disease.

"For better or worse, for richer and poorer, in sickness and in health, till death do you part." When the kids are sick, during times of unemployment, through a difficult pregnancy, in the event of lasting disability, "even then will I love you and care for you." When one is grumpy, when times are tough, when someone else seems more attractive, "even then will I stick by you." This is what the marital commitment means. It is sealed by a vow made to God. Only if we believe in the possibility and nobility of self-control can we even contemplate such a vow. Only if freedom exists, can marriage exist. Only if we can take responsibility for our own choices can marriage survive.

The political movement for homosexual "marriage," ironically, testifies to the truth of normal and traditional marriage, at least in one respect. Same sex couples rightly see the bond of committed normal married couples as somehow respectable and genuinely good. But they are blind to the deep roots of fertility, the complementarity in soul and body of the two sexes, and the necessity of giving oneself to the truly different, sexually different, "other" that give marriage its full meaning. Their own erotic friendships may be contrary to nature, but what good they do have is even more defective without a pledge to resist promiscuity and total reduction to mere pleasure. So a kind of parasitic homage is paid to actual marriage by this movement. It cannot, however, be justified in a republic founded on the laws of nature and of nature's God. And to call such partnerships marriage is to falsify the common language. One is reminded of one of Lincoln's jokes here. This is how he told it:

> "How many legs does a dog have, if you call a tail a leg?"
> "Five?"
> "Four; calling a tail a leg does not make it one."

So far, such legalization of same sex partnerships under the name "marriage" with the force of law has been the chiefly the action of judicial usurpation. Until 2009, no elected legislature had called a tail a leg. Nor had any popular referendum until 2012. Indeed, all relevant referenda had taken the contrary position, defining marriage as a tie between one man and one woman. one such popular vote yielded the same result as late as 2012.

When the Supreme Court in 2015 commanded all the States to treat Same Sex Marriage as a Civil right by a bare 5–4 majority, Chief Justice John Robeerts wrote this: "The majority's decision is an act of will, not legal judgment. The right it announces has no basis in the Constitution or this Court's precedent. The majority expressly disclaims judicial 'caution' and omits even a pretense of humility, openly relying on its desire to remake society according to its own 'new insight' into the "nature of injustice.' Ante, at 11, 23. As a result, the Court invalidates the marriage laws of more than half the States and orders the transformation of a social institution that has formed the basis of human society for millennia, for the Kalahari Bushmen and the Han Chinese, the Carthaginians and the Aztecs. Just who do we think we are?"

The unelected judges who have made other unions marriage have placed their will, and by implication, the authority of law, on the side of lies and inauthentic freedom. It is unclear what the American people's response will be as time goes on. But it will be a test of our character, however it turns out.

There is an evil spirit abroad today (it often comes to us through the internet and in film or on stage) that whispers to us, "the marital commitment doesn't mean much. You don't have to wait for marriage, or obey natural law, to enjoy sexual pleasure. If an inconvenient child is conceived, you may destroy it in the womb. If you are stressed in your marriage, you should be free to abandon spouse and children to find your own personal comfort." We justify heeding this voice by telling ourselves that our right to be happy, to be comfortable, trumps every other concern. When we undermine marriage, we tell ourselves that the *children* would be unhappy if *we* are not personally fulfilled. But the fact is that when we do this, we have refused the duty to place our children's happiness over our own comfort. If we won't make the sacrifices necessary to take care of our own children, how will they be taught to make any sacrifices for strangers? Or fellow citizens?

Tocqueville thought that there would never be a people both free and irreligious. We may wonder whether there can long be a people politically free and at the same time indifferent to marriage and careless of innocent children.

EDUCATING WORKERS FOR THE TWENTY-FIRST CENTURY

The state of public education in our country has been a growing concern for decades. Educators have been echoing the public outcry for reform, but somehow things never seem to get any better. Part of the reason is a fundamental flaw in what reformers think the goal of education should be. Today, many universities and an increasing number of high school and elementary schools are focused on one goal for education—to get a job. Increasingly, schools are judged only on the extent to which they properly prepare students to take their place in the world of the multinational corporations and government bureaucracies which will provide for them.

Americans used to combine moral consensus and stability with innovation and flexibility in economic matters. Now we teach moral uncertainty, or relativism, and are on the cusp of teaching a kind of timidity and narrow-mindedness in preparation for work. If we look to immediate job placement, not long-term job creation via enterprise and investment, we will have sacrificed growth for security, and we will have a future more like the mature, and slow-growth economies of Western Europe. Like those nations, we will also have nothing by way of national confidence or moral resolve to set against the threat of Radical Islamism, or whatever new enemy to human progress and dignity may arise.

'Workforce education' has formed an unholy alliance with multiculturalism and the new morality. We speak of "woke" corporations, for example. It has produced an emphasis on forming relativistic habits of mind and heart, because, in the opinion of educationists and corporate leaders, these workplaces must be free of the "divisive" arguments that might arise if someone says that some ways of life really are better than others. But such relativism implies a subversion of the possibility of reason and reflection reaching judgment in matters ethical and moral.

It is a counsel of despair about the very end of education, namely, some degree of human wisdom about human goods. It also means removing authority and respect from professors and classroom teachers, whose love is teaching and learning, and transferring them to administrators, economists, and bureaucrats, who claim to know how to plan for the "needs of the 21st Century."

But these planners have never successfully foreseen human needs. Their follies have made an economic and environmental wasteland of the riches of Eurasia, as may be seen by reviewing the experiments and enterprises of Stalin and his successors. Nor have they created wealth. They have only robbed Peter to pay Paul, and slowed the progress of human dynamism deployed in the pursuit of happiness.

Workforce education marks a radical change from the ways of our forefathers. As we have seen, in the past, students at all levels were educated chiefly to understand and to practice the principles that make a free society possible. They read history, literature, and moral treatises; some learned a foreign language and all a bit of mathematics. Having developed their capacity to think, many graduates were able to make important decisions about what is best, what is wise, and what is just, for themselves and society. By first being good humans, capable of reasoning for themselves, they were then able to exercise their minds in inventive ways to build up the vast, energetic, and wealthy economy the United States enjoys today.

We need to rethink the goals of education if our country is to survive. A democracy in which the public comes to think that one way of life is no better than any other, will soon judge everything by its price, including themselves, whom they will hardly value any more.

GOD IN EXILE

We have said that religious worship has always been the keystone of the arch of the American republic. Over the last forty years, however, God has been more and more exiled from our public life. He can't be supplicated in public schools. He can't be honored in public displays. He is generally unwelcome in our movies and TV shows, except those that mock the simple or hypocritical people who worship Him. The mention of God in the Pledge of Allegiance has been challenged in court.

It used to be a sign of character, or at least propriety, when a political official submitted his actions to the judgement of a higher being; now, in some circles, it is a cause of suspicion if a public man admits he prays.

Moral revolutions do not stand still. Thus we see that first comes the attack on moral restraint in the name of freedom, and then soon after comes, in the name of that same, now immoral, freedom, the denial that there can be freedom at all. Likewise, some begin by denying God so that man may be properly exalted. Man, they think, cannot be the greatest being, if there is a God. Is man not free, autonomous, unbounded by law or limit or even condition? One thinks of Ivan Karamazov here.

Soon, it happens that they deny that man has any soul. And yet, the soul knows it did not make itself and it knows that it desires to know more than itself, and feels that it is destined to something more than this world of matter.

In order that man may *not* have such immortal aspirations, which point beyond himself, (God forbid!) he must be conceived as soulless, a random swarm of atomic particles, without spirit, or will, or finally, freedom. Or so Dostoyevsky thought it out for us in Russia, more than a century ago when he wrote *The Brothers Karamazov*. Thus, in naïve America, caught up in Ivan's spiritual revolution, though innocent of the provenance of that thought from nihilist Europe, a few years ago an American Federal Court ordered Louisiana public schools to cease using an abstinence-only sex education program because it violated the separation of church and state by teaching that man is more than a beast!

Although the attack on the public role of religion opened with a handful of specific Supreme Court decisions, it now reaches deeply into the public mind. Even some pious Americans think that any public decision that conforms with a religious teaching or is advocated for reasons of religion might be un-American.

We Americans today sense that something is wrong, deeply wrong. All our recent trends, our liberation" from religion, our materialism and relativism, our sexual license, seem not to have made us happy. We are proud of our prosperity and our might in the world, unmatched in the long history of the civilizations earth has seen pass away. Yet, when we defend liberty and innocent life abroad, we are uncomfortably aware that we kill the unborn and practice license at home. We had thought of ourselves as the beacon of liberty, a "city on a hill." And the world had sometimes echoed that sentiment.

Now, faced with the promotion of the false face of freedom by our own citizens, some of us are speechless, incapable of giving reasons, silent, and ashamed of our silence, but not, of course, contented. But we are not altogether lost as a people. We have only to recall what made us a people, and to make it shine in our speech, in our deeds, and in all our lives. In order to become worthy of our freedom, worthy of our national might, and worthy of the burden of responsibility that that surpassing might places upon us, in a world filled with the poor, the vulnerable, and the innocent, we need only once again live by the Declaration of Independence.

We began this book asking you to take the Declaration to heart. In recent years, the legislature of New Jersey debated a law asking for public school children to commit a bit of the Declaration to memory, and to recite it each day in their classrooms. Here is what a contemporary statesman wrote in defense of this law:

If anything can be certain in history, it is that without the civic creed summarized in the opening of the Declaration, the United States would not exist as a free country. The Declaration gives the reasons for which the War of Independence was fought and expresses the motivation that enabled that war to be won. Since that day, the Declaration has been an indispensable foundation for a series of important struggles for justice in America, including of course the abolition of slavery.

Without the Declaration, I believe, these struggles would not have been won.

If we intend to keep alive in our children the knowledge of the true source of their dignity, we must be sure that their minds are formed in the light of the Declaration. Recitation of the key passages of the Declaration is a simple—and, one might even say self-evident—step toward this goal....

Contained in the Declaration are the seeds of an ethic of responsibility, for its acknowledgment of our obligations to God leads to the acknowledgment of our obligation to one another. The doctrine of dignified human equality under God provides the basis, therefore, for shaping character in our civic culture in such a way that we eschew being serfs and subjects but at the same time refuse to be bullies and despots. A generation raised on the Declaration will insist we owe to our fellow citizen the same respect that we demand from him.

The Declaration is not merely a powerful tool for spiritual and moral motivation—it is probably an irreplaceable one....

The schoolchild who reads the Declaration, thinks about it and is moved to give it his assent in however simple a form, is a symbol of the American citizen of any age or intelligence. The full life of citizenship in America is a life lived in reflection on the truths of our founding, continued assent to those truths and continued resolve to act in light of them.

This is the challenge of liberty.

– Ambassador Alan Keyes, May 27, 2000

The legislation did not pass. What should we, the citizens, do now?

BIBLIOGRAPHY

The Constitution of the United States of America and the Constitution of the State of California. Sacramento: California Legislature Assembly, 1997.

Inaugural Addresses of the Presidents of the United States. Washington, D.C.: United States Government Printing Office, 1961.

Adams, James Truslow. *The March of Democracy: A History of the United States.* New York: Charles Scribner's Sons, 1933.

Amos, Gary T. *Defending the Declaration.* Brentwood, Tennessee: Wolgemuth & Hyatt, 1989.

Anderson, Nancy Scott and Dwight G. *The Generals: Ulysses S. Grant and Robert E. Lee.* New York: Alfred A. Knopf, 1988.

Bailyn, Bernard. *The Ideological Origins of the American Revolution.* Cambridge, Massachusetts: Belknap Press of Harvard University Press, 1967.

Bruckberger, R.L. *Image of America.* New York: The Viking Press, 1959.

Basler, Roy P., ed. *Abraham Lincoln: His Speeches and Writings.* Cleveland: The World Publishing Company, 1953, 54 editions.

Budziszewski, J. *Written on the Heart: The Case for Natural Law.* Downers Grove, Illinois: InterVarsity Press, 1997.

Carson, Clarence B. *The Rebirth of Liberty: The Founding of the American Republic 1760–1800.* Irvington-on-Hudson, NY: The Foundation for Economic Education, Inc., 1976.

Coolidge, Calvin. *Foundations of the Republic: Speeches and Addresses.* New York: Charles Scribner's Sons, 1926.

— *The Price of Freedom: Speeches and Addresses.* New York: Charles Scribner's Sons, 1924.

Corwin, Edward S. *The "Higher Law" Background of American Constitutional Law.* Ithaca: Cornell University Press, 1971.

Cruden, Robert. *The Negro in Reconstruction*. Englewood Cliffs, New Jersey: Prentice-Hall, Inc., 1969.

Diamond, Martin. *The Founding of the Democratic Republic*. Itasca, Illinois: F.E. Peacock Publishers, Inc., 1981.

Franklin, John Hope. *From Slavery to Freedom: A History of Negro Americans*. New York: Vintage Books, 1969.

—*Reconstruction: After the Civil War*. Chicago: The University of Chicago Press, 1961.

Grob, Gerald N. and Robert N. Beck, eds. *American Ideas: Source Readings in the Intellectual History of the 161 United States, Vol. I: Foundations (1629–1865)*. New York: The Free Press, 1963.

Hamilton, Alexander, John Jay and James Madison. *The Federalist*. New York: The Modern Library, 1937.

Hickok, Eugene W., ed. *The Bill of Rights, Original Meaning and Current Understanding*. Charlottesville: University Press of Virginia, 1991.

Holmes, Leon. "What Shall We Be? A Study of the Political Thought of Three Black Americans." Unpublished doctoral dissertation, Duke University: 1980.

Horwitz, Robert H., ed. *The Moral Foundations of the American Republic*. Charlottesville: University Press of Virginia, 1979.

Hutson, Cecil Kirk. *The California Civil Rights Initiative: Restoring Equality Under the Law*. Sacramento, California: Assembly Republican Caucus, Office of Policy Research, 1996.

Jaffa, Harry V. *Crisis of the House Divided: An Interpretation of the Issues in the Lincoln-Douglas Debates*. Seattle: University of Washington Press, 1973.

— *Equality and Liberty, Theory and Practice in American Politics*. New York: Oxford University Press, 1965.

Jefferson, Thomas. *Writings*. New York: Literary Classics of the United States, 1984.

Johannsen, Robert W., ed. *The Lincoln-Douglas Debates of 1858*. New York: Oxford University Press, 1965.

Keyes, Alan L. *Masters of the Dream: The Strength and Betrayal of Black America*. New York: Quill, William Morrow, 1995.

Link, Arthur S. *Woodrow Wilson and the Progressive Era, 1910–1917.* New York: Harper Torchbooks, Harper & Row, 1954.

Lincoln, Abraham. *Abraham Lincoln: His Speeches and Writings*, ed. Roy P. Basler. Cleveland: The World Publishing Company, 1946.

Lincoln, Abraham and Stephen A. Douglas. *The Lincoln-Douglas Debates of 1858*, ed. Robert W. Johannsen. New York: Oxford University Press, 1965.

— *Political Debates Between Hon. Abraham Lincoln and Hon. Stephen A. Douglas, in the Celebrated Campaign of 1858, in Illinois; Including the Preceding speeches of each, at Chicago, Springfield, etc.; also, the Two Great Speeches of Mr. Lincoln in Ohio, in 1859, as Carefully Prepared by the Reporters of each Party, and Published at the Times of Their Delivery.* Columbus: Follett, Foster and Company, 1860.

Locke, John. *The Second Treatise of Government*, ed. Thomas P. Peardon. Indianapolis: Bobbs-Merrill Educational Publishing, 1952.

Lutz, Donald S. *The Origins of American Constitutionalism.* Baton Rouge: Louisiana State University Press, 1988.

McDonald, Forrest. *Novus Ordo Seclorum: The Intellectual Origins of the Constitution.* Lawrence, Kansas: University Press of Kansas, 1985.

Madison, James. *The Complete Madison, His Basic Writings*, ed. Saul K, Padover. New York: Harper & Brothers, 1953.

Maier, Pauline. *American Scripture: The Making of the Declaration of Independence.* 1998.

Malone, Dumas. *The Story of the Declaration of Independence.* New York: Oxford University Press, 1954.

Morison, Samuel Eliot. *The Oxford History of the American People.* New York: Oxford University Press, 1965.

Morris, Richard B., ed. *Significant Documents in United States History, Volume II, 1898–1968.* New York: Van Nostrand Reinhold Company, 1969.

Padover, Saul K., ed. *The Story of the Declaration of Independence.* New York: Oxford University Press, 1954.

Rahe, Paul A. *Republics Ancient and Modern, Vol. III, Inventions of Prudence:*

Constituting the American Regime. Chapel Hill: University of North Carolina Press, 1994.

Ryan, John A. and Francis J. Boland. *Catholic Principles of Politics.* New York: The Macmillan Company, 1940.

Skrentny, John David. *The Ironies of Affirmative Action.* Chicago: University of Chicago Press, 1996.

de Tocqueville, Alexis. *Democracy in America,* ed. Phillips Bradley. New York: Vintage Books, 1957.

West, Thomas G. *Vindicating the Founders.* Lanham, Maryland: Rowman & Littlefield Publishers, 1997.

Wills, Garry. *Cincinnatus, George Washington and the Enlightenment.* Garden City, New York: Doubleday, 1984.

Wise, John. "A Vindication of the Government of New-England Churches: Chapter II (Boston, 1717)," in *American Ideas,* ed. Gerald N. Grob and Robert N. Beck. New York: The Free Press, 1963.